A WOMAN IN CANADA

BY

MRS. GEORGE CRAN

PHILADELPHIA

J. B. LIPPINCOTT COMPANY

LONDON: JOHN MILNE

1910

LIST OF ILLUSTRATIONS

PORTRAIT OF THE AUTHOR . . .	*Frontispiece*	
A LAND OF MOUNTAIN AND LAKE . .	*Facing page*	16
AN OLD QUEBEC STREET	,, ,,	20
THE SETTLED EAST : OTTAWA . . .	,, ,,	24
THE WOMAN FARMER	,, ,,	35
MY HOSTESS AT CALEDONIA SPRINGS .	,, ,,	40
CALEDONIA SPRINGS HOTEL . . .	,, ,,	42
EXPERIMENTAL FARM AT BRANDON . .	,, ,,	47
A TINY LOG CABIN	,, ,,	53
CATTLE BY THE POND AT CALEDONIA SPRINGS	,, ,,	58
OTTO THE GUIDE AT LEANCHOIL . .	,, ,,	63
"A BIG FELLOW"	,, ,,	66
PREPARING LUNCH	,, ,,	77
FISHING : "LANDED"	,, ,,	85
BRINGING HOME THE MOOSE HEAD . .	,, ,,	87
SKINNING HEAD OF MOOSE . . .	,, ,,	90
THE PRAIRIE	,, ,,	96
GRAIN ELEVATORS	,, ,,	100
WOMEN ARE SCARCE IN THE NORTH-WEST	,, ,,	115
NEAR LEANCHOIL, WHERE OTTO LIVES .	,, ,,	128

LIST OF ILLUSTRATIONS

INTERIOR OF A LOG CABIN . . . *Facing page* 135

WHERE REAL SPORT MAY BE HAD . . ,, ,, 152

MOOSE . . . . ,, ,, 166

THE FRINGE OF THE WILD . . . ,, ,, 178

"MR. MUGGINS" . . . . . ,, ,, 191

OUR CAMP ON MALIGNE LAKE . . . ,, ,, 195

"MR. MUGGINS" GETS A RIDE. . . ,, ,, 206

OUR DINNER-TABLE . . . . . ,, ,, 219

MOUNT ROBSON . . . . . ,, ,, 235

THE PACIFIC PROVINCE . . . . ,, ,, 251

PINES IN HIGH WATER: KAMLOOPS LAKE,
BRITISH COLUMBIA . . . ,, ,, 269

THE IONE SONG . . . . . ,, ,, 280

A WOMAN IN CANADA

CHAPTER I

FOREWORD

LET me beg any one who does not like "I's" to avoid this book. It is full of them.

The first time I went to Canada I spent the days of preparation for departure in being very sorry for myself. I could not think why I had said I would go. There was no need for it. I wasn't going to settle there, or invest money. I was only going on a visit with friends, and as the date of sailing grew near they noticed my depression. "Was I home-sick?" "No, not yet." "Was I a bad sailor?" "No, not specially." "What was the matter, then?" Under pressure of questioning the trouble burst forth. Canada was an ugly, cold, icebergy place; it had miles of flat wheat; it had no flowers; it was ugly, and I hated ugliness. Would they understand if I was morose during my visit, and believed that I loved them and only hated the country?

Such a way as they teased me!

"Yes! they would understand—indeed they would. And if I wanted flowers very badly they would take me to a marsh on a moor where purple flags grew, and frogs crooned at night."

Goodness knows what idea I had of the country— no literature I had ever read had forced an impression of beauty into my brain; it talked of so many bushels to the acre, so many acres to the farm, so many feet of snow to this month, so many days of drought to this, and so on. One book left a vivid picture of the hardships of homesteading, another told of the political value of the country, but none that I had ever seen talked intimately of the scenery or of the days' happenings other than commercially. I knew what grew there because I had seen the Coronation Arch. *Hiawatha* hung in the memory only as a jargon of interminable names cleverly arranged in trochaics. Lamentable, horrible, unintelligent as it sounds, there is the fact of my ignorance. It has one advantage which I make haste to point out. I have at any rate viewed Canada through my own eyes, no one else's. And I venture to believe that it would strike hundreds of my fellow-Britons as it did me, especially, perhaps, women Britons. .

I believe that the average Englishman keeps a

small but warm corner of his heart for the word
"colonies." Pride of possession counts for nearly
all the warmth in that corner. When he looks there
he finds a few vague notions lying loose, just any-
how, all warm, all prized in a careless, happy way;
but none of them loved in laborious detail. The
vague notions spell vague things to him. India
generally spells, I think, "Elephants a-pilin' teak,"
and whisky-pegs; Africa, diamonds and "Kaffirs";
Australia, sheep and cricket; Canada, wheat and discomfort. It sounds foolish and almost impossible,
but I believe that for the average Briton that is a
fairly accurate description of what the Colonies
amount to. The word "Canada" brings to his brain
pictures of Liverpool receiving vast cargoes of wheat
and distributing them over the country at a lower
price than the home farmer demands. It also arouses
dim visions of privations endured most impatiently
by sundry of his friends who have gone out to
Canada to settle, and hurried back incontinently
because the young country did not contain all the
comforts of the old. The name of Canada is to
average Englishmen an empty word—as a nation
we do not realize her beauty, her power, or her proud
resentment of our ignorance of both.

If the average Englishman regards Canada as a

vast plain of alternate snow and wheat, or else as a speculative habitation for spare capital, never as a beautiful, spacious home, the bulk of Canadians, in their turn, regard England as a high-spirited ward is liable to regard a wealthy guardian of cranky temper—a guardian whose powers of control must terminate with the ward's maturity, and who will probably be dearly loved from the perspective of release; but who, meanwhile, is to be endured, and considerably grumbled at. The traveller from these islands to the big Dominion is apt to start out with the erroneous idea that his nationality will give him prestige over there, will excuse, perhaps idealize, any eccentricity on his part, and any ignorance of his destination. This apprehension is inevitably subject to many shocks, and his pride of race is violently thrust back upon him during his sojourn in Canada. The Canadian, generally speaking, regards the Englishman with little of his own regard for himself, and does not share his pride in the little island home whence he comes. The man who is proud of the past is unlikely to find much in common with the man who is proud of the future.

"See what we have done," cries the Englishman, and "See what we are going to do," cries the Canadian!

Excellent prides, both of them; in the vital energy which impels the latter, one is prone to overlook the element of uncertainty it contains.

"Your country is worn out!" said a young Ontarian to me. "Your roads have hedges, and are kept like park-walks; every hill is labelled 'Caution'; every turning has a sign-post to tell which way to go. Your very roads nurse and pamper the intelligence out of a man. Why, I'd soon learn to rely on signs instead of the sun for my direction if I lived there; and I'd forget to shoot if I had your country; every acre of bush has a 'trespass-board' in it instead of something for the pot. Your country is worn out."

The narrowness of outlook displayed in these remarks will be derided by the superficial reader; but there is, in fact, reason in the view taken by so many Canadians. We are in danger of becoming a nation of cities, an urban race unfitted to wrestle with the wild. Only they judge us as already unfit who are, as yet, only becoming unfit.

The population of Canada, a little less than that of London alone, is drawn from many sources; its prairies are tilled by Italians, Germans, Swedes, Danes, Galicians, Doukobours and Americans, besides the French and English. In British Columbia

Asiatic labour swarms; the costly, excellent "boy" is at once the heartburn and the godsend of the Pacific province; he is felt to be a menace and a necessity, and is regarded with the oddest mixture of distrust and gratitude. That same uncertainty of attitude, in a modified degree, obtains towards the French element in Canada, and towards the powerful and yearly growing contingent from the States. The general idea over here is that Canada is peopled with Britons, with a certain admixture of old French blood; that the two get on capitally, and unite in adoring England and everything English. Never was such folly. Canada welcomes to her shores every man of every race who will work her soil and obey her laws; she draws her people from every nation, and the English settler has *not* proved himself the best man. The Italians and Galicians show infinitely greater adaptability, greater industry, greater patience. A certain proportion of Canada's English settlers has, unfortunately, been drawn from the wastrels of our upper classes, and a large proportion from the poor. As yet the average decent, hardworking, intelligent middle-class Englishman has not made his mark on public opinion. Oddly enough—and this is a fact—the Englishwoman in Canada is everywhere welcomed and valued. In the

14

North-West, where wives are scarce, a work of Empire awaits the woman of breed and endurance who will settle on the prairie homesteads and rear their children in the best traditions of Britain. Canada can do with citizens who put honour before wealth; and Britain greatly needs, if she only knew it, a loyal leaven in her greatest colony.

Will I ever forget my first sight of that lovely country? All the elfin beauty of dusk was there to glamour the hour; there was a smell of land warm and piney on the breeze; after days of brine sprayed bitterly to the nostrils there was delight in it; all the happy langour of green growing things, all the fruitful essences of earth soothed the senses in that breeze blowing from the land. We crowded up on deck to lean over the waters. Overhead the moon swung between tiny clouds like a censer sometimes dimmed by its own smoke; away on our left stretched the great St. Lawrence. On the right a long patch of indigo broke the sky-line; in the heart of that line sparkled Rimouski. After leaving the mails we steamed away up the vast moonlit river, passing between the sentinel spires that fringe her banks to the city of spires, perched on their historic heights, the many-towered fairy city which broke upon our vision in the unearthly dawnlight—a sight to be remembered for all days, poignant with mystery, with charm. Here I was, ushered into the "ugly icebergy place" through the portals of a mighty sunlit river; transfigured with emotion as we swept past the country of Evangeline, *Sunshine of Saint Eulalie*, realizing for the first time the beauty and truth of the descriptions read so lightly in far-off school-days. Why do people skip descriptions in books? One can travel the world over, in an arm-chair, and know the aspect of every land, if one only would read with patience in the printed page. So, rebuked, enlightened, did I come to Canada. For evermore her name will spell to me a picture of mountain and valley, of lake and river, of fruitful orchards and quaint young townships; it will bring to my nostrils the smell of her, which is the smell of pine and cedar. My ears will strain to hear again the noon-song of the crickets and vesper of the frogs. That is the picture of Canada as I know her now, as all know her who love that rich and splendid land of promise, which only awaits for the "open sesame" of honest and ungrudging labour to pour her wealth into the world.

That first visit, which taught me so much, was confined to Quebec and Ontario, the big eastern provinces which contain four of the seven great cities

A Land of Mountain and Lake

Page 16

in the whole Colony. Guess, then, the prospect
unfolded in a second visit which was to take me
across to the Pacific coast, over the famed prairies,
through the Rocky Mountains and British Columbia.
I should see the lonely prairie farms, should see the
world's wheat brought to harvest; should touch the
fringe of the wild, and learn from the lips of pioneers
the hardships and rewards of their courage.

Here, in this little book, I propose to set forth
a picture of Canada as I saw her; I, raw from
the Mother Country, with nothing to hope for,
nothing to gain, no one to profit, nothing to make
out of a good report and nothing to fear from ill
report. Perhaps I should say something here of
the terms of my second journey. Seeing that the
Canadian Government sent me across the country it
might seem that I was bound to speak well of it, but
as a matter of fact I do not feel handicapped by any
such idea. The Dominion Government paid my
travelling expenses, the Canadian Pacific and
Canadian Northern Railways gave me passes over
their lines; but beyond these courtesies I went
unpaid, and acted heartily on the final word of
advice from official sources: "Speak the truth, we
can stand it." I wonder if it sounds too noble to
say that without such a free hand I should not have

gone. It is true, however. It would have been too tiresome. A certain proportion of the matter here set forth has already appeared in article form in the *Bystander*, the *Daily Chronicle*, the *Lady*, the *Crown*, the *Standard of Empire* and *Madame*. My acknowledgments are due to the editors of these papers for their courtesy in permitting me to adapt what was necessary.

I have in nowise endeavoured to write a travel book—nasty dowdy things they are, full of fact and figures, written by people with tidy minds, and packed with information and help for every emergency that can possibly arise in the career of the least accomplished traveller, and bursting with answers to every question that could possibly be asked by the most intelligent ones. This is only a series of snapshots, offered with ragged edges—unglazed, unmounted, unframed, rapid, disconnected reproductions of this picture and of that which burned into the memory in the six and a half months which is all I have ever spent in Canada. If I had spent six and a half years in the country, if I had worked and played, grieved and rejoiced, loved and hated on its soil among its people, then, perhaps, I might make some effort at presenting a coherent substantial book of reference and analysis; but such an effort now would be an impertinence, and one which I respect Canada too much to offer. There is a heresy buried in that confession, a social heresy, a bad principle, a dangerous theory; one that would set sincerity before polish, and do civilization a lot of damage; but it is not my business to point it out. What I realize is that, having travelled over one of our great Colonies, along a track that has been trodden scores of times before by people who can write much better than I can, I am attempting to write of it again; Heaven help me.

Strange the fascination that land possesses! I am not in the least peculiar in owning to it, countless men and women have told me the same thing, and a fact which is well known to all students of immigration over there is that ninety per cent. of the new settlers who put in a year or two, fail and leave in disgust, *come back*. They can't help it—any more than I can now help the painful desire which catches me by the throat as August draws near, to pace again the deck of the out-going steamer impatient to devour time, while the Marconi machine coughs out messages to unseen vessels, spluttering blue sparks the while; impatient to see the wild maidenhair again upon the mountains, the little wild orchids coloured like copper in firelight, to hear the frogs

chant evensong, and crickets wake the day. I can
neither stay nor ignore reconstruction of the journey,
and I long to pass Belle Isle in a drenching fog with
a tireless syren—to breast the gulf, and sail proudly
like a queen-swan to Rimouski in the sunset; I long
to feel the screws shiver as we set forth again for
Quebec, leaving Rimouski an indigo line throbbing
with firefly lights; I long once more to come to
Quebec in the dawn—and at that moment always in
my longing I begin to be glad, like a lover who has
come to his own. High poised against clear skies
I see once more the Camelot of Canada—Quebec of
the heights and spires, grey, quaint, beautiful Quebec,
hung up between heaven and earth over her spark-
ling river; I rattle over her stony streets in a calèche;
I see the big grasshoppers, like butterflies, among
the chicory flowers beside the city ramparts; I stand
in reverence before a hero's monument upon the
plains of Abraham, and in wonder before the view
at the Château Frontenac. In all the loved, scented
beauty of rose-time in England I feel a reiteration
of that longing to be in Canada again; I want to
linger in Ottawa, the garden-city; to see Winnipeg
again lying flat on the prairie, with the sky-line an
amber belt about her loins at sunset; to watch the
green snakes gliding in and out among the grass

tufts; to see the log-fences and lonely wooden shacks. It is the toll exacted from all who have once been to Canada, unexpected but inevitable—this strange attachment. A curious feeling, not a sentimental impulse, but a queer tugging at the heart-strings which has its origin in emotion of some sort. I am no musician, and so cannot describe in the terms of the perfect Wagnerite what I mean when I speak of the "ache" of music—I mean that feeling of suspense which catches you when a melodious phrase is heard, and you know another must follow, similar, yet not the same, a sort of answer or completion of what went before; and the "ache" of music is that sensation of suspense, of waiting, of desire which holds the ear and heart unsatisfied till the completing phrase occurs. Any musician reading this will smile because I describe a common enough occurrence in melody without knowing its technical term. But lovers of music, unlearned like myself, will understand what I mean when I say that Canada appeals to me like the first phrase in a melody; it leaves one charmed, unsatisfied, desiring more.

I was asked on my second journey to regard the country from a woman's standpoint as much as possible; to study the lives of the Englishwomen settled there; to form my own opinion as to their happiness, their usefulness, their success or failure as settlers and wives of settlers; to discover if possible in what ways they could make money for themselves without having to wait for menfolk to bring them or send for them. For the Dominion Government is aware that England is overcrowded with women, and that her own prairie lands are crying for them by the thousand. Canada wants women of breed and endurance, educated, middle-class gentlewomen, and these are not the women to come out on the off-chance of getting married. They may be induced to come to the country if they can farm or work in some way to secure their absolute independence. They want, every nice woman wants, to be free to undertake marriage as a matter of choice, not of necessity. I feel persuaded that if the daughters of professional men in Great Britain could feel that there were possibilities of money-making in the Colonies for them, as well as for men, they would go out and prosper. They would not choose to compete in Great Britain, where the fight is severe; and once they settled in the North-West I believe that a large number would ultimately throw in their lot with the bachelor farmers of the prairie and British Columbia. Every woman who goes out to Canada makes it easier for the other women there. I would not recommend any one to go to the cities, they are overcrowded already; the eastern provinces, too, are fairly settled, but there is room for hundreds on the prairies, in Manitoba, that is to say, and Saskatchewan and Alberta, as also there is in British Columbia, the great province where climatic conditions are so different from those of the rest of Canada as to make it seem another kingdom! Like Gaul, Canada is divided into three parts—there are the settled eastern provinces, Ontario, Quebec, Nova Scotia and New Brunswick; then the great tract of prairie land divided into the three provinces aforementioned, Manitoba, Saskatchewan and Alberta, where the flat soil is a deep black loam, a quick fertile vegetable mould, where the wheat grows and the ranches are; where the track of buffalo may still be seen, where the eye may roam for days of travelling without finding a tree or bush. Then there is the third part of Canada, British Columbia, which begins in the Rocky Mountains and stretches down to the Pacific seas, where the cedars grow to immense proportions, where all growth is lush and rank, where snows give place to a rainy season, where the rivers are full of salmon and the forests full of deer. I was picking strawberries in the open in one of the valleys of British Columbia last autumn, and three days later the train I was in was snowed up in the Maple Creek blizzard—such differences of climate are to be found in that vast continent we call Canada.

I think that elementary division of the country is helpful in trying to picture it to oneself. First the east—settled, civilized, almost *blasé;* then the middle—wild, flat, fertile, full of potential riches, and even that is settling so quickly that its great curse, the curse of loneliness, is passing away; and last the west—beautiful, luxuriant, largely unexploited, heavily timbered, with gold in all its rivers and fruit orchards in its valleys.

The climate of Canada is magnificent, extremer in heat and cold than England, but dry and bracing. The conditions are primitive, and of every one but the capitalist manual labour is demanded as the first necessity of life.

CHAPTER II

A WOMAN FARMER AND AN EXPERIMENTAL FARM

WE have sailed the stately river. Here are Montreal, the Customs, the drunken telegraph posts, the hum of welcome, the bustle of landing. I make straight for the great Canadian Pacific Railway building to ask for a pass, and am struck with the happy atmosphere that there prevails. One Mr. Stitt studies my letters and myself, then makes it his business to present the staff. I learn from one man of the picturesqueness of the Indians, their legends, their history, he is such an enthusiast in his study that I long for nothing so much as to go and live among them, learn them, write of them; but he is whisked away, and there passes before my marvellous eyes, a succession of enthusiasts as interesting. The voice of wisdom speaks from Mr. Hayter Reid, the hotel enthusiast, telling me in chosen phrases of the wonders of life in the mountains, so that I burn to go there without any more delay and spend the rest of life fishing in the lakes, hunting, trapping, riding. Then a wheat enthusiast quarrels with them both about the superiority of wheat growing as a pastime to Indian lore and hotel life; as he talks I hear the rustle of grain in the sun with the wind among it, I yearn utterly to stand upon the prairies and lose myself in wheat. Then comes George Ham, "The only George Ham in the world," and he is witty and warm, and silent and cold, all in ten seconds or so. I understand, now I am among these men, why the Canadian Pacific Railway is the great, successful power it is. It is managed by picked souls, happy, genial, brilliant souls.

Seeing it is yet early morning and I am a stranger in the land, I ask them what I can see in the afternoon. The Indian enthusiast wants me to go to Caughnawaga, the Indian village, but the others advise me to take a "round" ticket to Lachine and shoot the rapids on the St. Lawrence. With the rustle of the Atlantic and throb of engines still in my ears I feel I am a little weary of water and make demur. I ask if it is dangerous, and the enthusiasts smile one and all. "There had never been an accident and they had been shot thousands of times." So I wander away to the Grand Trunk station and take my "round" ticket. I crowd into the train with the multitude and am carried at last into the open; it is good to feel the city behind me and the hedgeless country all around. A large proportion of the crowd gets off at Lachine, a heavy thunderstorm comes on, and we wait on the wharf herded uncomfortably under a tiny shelter. Presently the fat old *Empress* rolls up; she is a white boat with a curious engine which carries two exalted iron arms in her middle; when the engine works these arms wave up and down in a fashion that excites in me an inexplicable pity; they look so futile, so unintelligent, and so deplorably patient—like a very tired woman rocking a child that will not sleep, or a soldier heliographing to some one that cannot see. I am not sure if all the crowd is able to get on at Lachine, there is a great rush and I am swept on the front of it; I find myself tumbling over a small boy and his crushed cries make me angry, I don't want to hurt him and the people behind make me. I try to lift him but cannot stoop, it is an eager crowd and the gangway is narrow. Presently he is squeezed through the railing and falls into the water. It must be much more comfortable for him than under my feet. I am swept on deck and begin to breathe again, the boy is fished out at once and greatly coddled and petted, he deserves it, poor little person, and we set out for the rapids. The *Empress* has come from Ottawa, and is fairly well loaded with luggage and passengers. All of us, who can, crowd into the bows to see the great feat accomplished, despite the rain, which makes an ineffable freshness in the air after a hot, close day. It is evening; I entertain lively hopes of seeing a brilliant river sunset as soon as the rain ceases. Sitting on a little wooden chair in the crowd I study the ugly blouse and untidy belt in front of me, congratulating myself that neither can block out my view of the sky, although they can, and do, any hope of seeing the rapids. A man next me begins to talk loftily of "Colonials"; he is an Englishman, I regret to say, with bulgy blue eyes and a waxed moustache and shiny red cheeks; he says he is over on a patriotic mission. I hope he is lying. That is the type of man who spoils England for Canadians. I get up and squeeze over to the other side, where a rough-looking Ontarian with kind eyes gives me his chair, telling me to climb up on it and "look there." I climb, and look. All across the wide St. Lawrence from far green bank to far green bank boils and fumes a line of breakers. It seems incredible that any boat can pass across these rocks and currents in safety. The man holds my arm to steady me, the motion of the boat is growing rapid, everybody is craning to see, we are just above the rapids. Mighty forces are dragging for our lives this way and that, here a whirlpool, there an angry scurry of waves rolling backward as I have seen them roll at Niagara in a flux of currents. I look up at the wheels, two men are steering, there are two wheels; the men are looking fixedly ahead, a great concentration of attention in pose and glance. An old lady near me hides her face, saying, "Oh, who is at the hellum?" The man who had given me his chair grips my arm tighter—we curve this way and that, intricately steered, and then we sweep terribly, resistlessly, over the fall into the maelstrom below. As we go I hear a crack. . . . I look up, the front wheel is flapping helplessly, the men are looking *frightened.* Another man rushes forward, he pulls the engine bell quickly, turns to the wheel, tries it and then all of them rush away.

They have left the bridge—something is wrong.

I look at the rough man, he still has my arm, his face is dead white; he says, "I have four children on board." The boat is moving horribly. Once she hits something and slides away on a current. I see we are in a hollow and ask, "Why is the river scooped out like this?" The man answers, "We are in the rapids, the rocks make it hollow." I see two sailors come from below and run like monkeys up an iron ladder; they disappear to the back of the boat. I hear shouts, people begin to realize, they rush to the sides and look over. . . . I look at the boats, there are not nearly enough, besides they wouldn't be any use, there are not enough life-belts to go round that crowd. They have reversed the engines to hold up against the current, the patient arms work up and down. Presently the man who is giving the engine orders smiles palely down upon us and signals again to the engines. We begin to move forward, he has four men working the helm from the back, and he gives them the direction with his hand from the bridge. So, very slowly, we come to Montreal. In the middle of the rapids, the steering gear had broken. For a while we have been in deadly peril, now it is over I know it has been very interesting.

I read a description of the Indian reserve Caughnawaga in the *Daily Express*, by Mr. Hambleton, afterwards, and it was so picturesque that I linger to quote part of it—

A jumbled, scattered collection of houses of wood and stone, a near neighbourhood of semi-wild, semi-cultivated land, a people with the dull, dead features of a nation without an ideal and without a future, a village in which past and present clash in strange, eerie silence—there you have Kahnawake—"near the rapids"— and shadows of men of the Five Nations.

Caughnawaga (to use the modern spelling) is but a few miles up the river from Montreal, but it is a leap back through two hundred and fifty years of history without parallel, history which tells of the gradual tightening of the white man's grip, and the dominance of the white man's faith. . . .

The jingling of civilizations is borne upon you with forceful persistence the moment you step ashore from the ferry. The main street of the village is broad, and the quality of its surface is fully equal to that of the average street in Montreal; but the resemblance ends there. A neat little hotel bids the visitor welcome, but the white stranger may not make his home in Caughnawaga. There are the same knots of playing, laughing children, yet the call of mother to child comes from one who passes down the street in silent aloofness from the present.

As she goes by, the young squaw pulls her black shawl more closely round the shoulders, and from under the big straw hat dark eyes gleam with a glitter vaguely reminiscent of the camp-fire. . . .

The Caughnawaga of to-day is not imposing, but the view from its shores is a delight painted with the bold, broad stroke of the master. It is such a scene as rivals, even if it does not excel, that from the "look-out" on Mount Royal. From the dim grey-blue of the mountains where Ottawa and St. Lawrence join their waters, eastward to the veil of smoke hanging over the city, the scene is one of softly-blending, ever-shifting colour, of restless industry and profound peace.

Swiftly, relentlessly, the great river rushes onward past the Indian village, eager to bring countless machines into life ere its course be run to the sea. Westward, where the St. Lawrence broadens into Lake St. Louis, a horde of panting launches dance and leap through the waves; and there, where the waters catch the glow of the flaming sky, diamond and ruby flash in twinkling light the eternal presence of the past. It is the scene which the Indian sees day by day from the reserve which is the white man's gift. He loves it all, but it is to him the water of Tantalus—unattainable. It is the land over which he once held sway.

When I got to the station the next day to start my westward journey, a little lonely, George Ham was there with a word to the conductor for my comfort, and a hand-clasp so friendly and unexpected that it wakes a grateful glow to this day. I clamber into the car, and could wish our English travelling were as easy. The cars are lofty and spacious, each seat is a separate arm-chair by the window, which may be wheeled into any position, and is the essence of comfort. The cars roll swiftly and very smoothly; the windows are vast sheets of plate glass, offering an uninterrupted view of the passing country. The ventilating arrangements are perfect, only the Canadian idea of ventilation is heat before freshness, never freshness and warmth as well if you can get it, therefore the ventilating arrangements appeal to me as being of little avail. A handsome carpet runs the length of the car, which is a glorified edition of Pullman as we know him, and the only grief I find in the whole arrangement is the perspective of tin bowls. One is placed by every chair, and some of the passengers make pestilential use of them. A boy passes to and fro at intervals with fruit, chocolate, or newspapers, and the porter is ready to bring tea at any moment and brush one's coat and boots before alighting. The train travels steadily, pulling up at a little station now and then with a deep contralto whistle. Near me a fellow-passenger tells the eternal story of England's coldness to her colony, Canada's patience and long-suffering; I listen indifferent well. Here is passing the landscape I love : here is a belt of maples, there a patch of golden-rod glistening in the sun, when the train slackens I can hear the crickets sing. My happiness is too deep to be pierced by this aged grievance, I refuse to be plunged in thankless argument. I watch the country whirl away from our wheels; I watch it, and grow conscious of a certain hunger. Something is not there that I love, and I do not know what it is. We pass field after field of maize, buckwheat, oats and pasture. The maize, always called corn here, is infinitely graceful. Its leaves hang from tall stalks like satin streamers of green ribbon; on top floats a plume of pale floss silk, tipped with brown. The buckwheat grows thick and short; it waves its tiny flowers in the wind, and sheds a perfume more fragrant and delicious than can be

imagined. Every farm, as we pass it, has wooden barns in proportion to its size and success. The fields are divided by log fences, which the cattle destroy with their horns; on the richer farms wire fences are used, more useful and lasting if less picturesque. I look at them idly. Suddenly I know what I miss. It is the snug hedges of England, where ragged robins are blooming now, and where soon the hips and haws will shine bright red; the hedges that grow so thick and high that the lanes run like little damp avenues between. This country is vaster, less closely partitioned. Over each small station that we pass is clearly written its name, the number of miles travelled since we left Montreal, and the number yet to be run before we reach Ottawa. I am bound for a farm of six hundred acres managed by a woman. I have never known a woman farmer before, and am not sure what to expect.

The train pulls up at Caledonia Springs, and my hostess runs to meet me. I look at her with curiosity which becomes interest; she has a knowledgable face, and wears middle-age with that dignity which comes of self-trust, moreover she is beautiful and dresses becomingly. I am at ease in her company, and she has the manner of the world; as she entertains me I realize that she has travelled far and remembered much, a woman whose brain has not yet ceased to grow, who has the charm of undisplayed experience in conversation.

After lunch we walk about the farm—she talks to herself rather than to me, her enthusiasm is too great to wait for questions.

"Come to the corn patch, I don't think any one has a better crop," and we walk up the cart track, with the grasshoppers flying before our feet. On every side there are signs of careful farming—here and there heaps of compost, the ditches have been cleaned, there are incredibly few weeds. Through the wire gate we pass into the "corn patch," there are sixteen acres of it and it looks like a young forest; under the tall spikes of feathery bloom and green ribbon leaves we lose the sun and sky. It is cool and fresh among the corn.

"It must average eight or nine feet," she says, "and this is only the 25th of August. It will grow much more yet, when the grain is nearly glazed it will be cut for silage."

I am looking at the fat ears on the thick stalks, each one tufted with a plume of pinky-green floss silk turning brown. Each stalk has many ears, we have no maize in England and this is the first time I have seen it growing close.

"What is silage?" I ask. My ignorance weighs upon me. "It is the same to this as hay is to grass," she answers. The whole stalk is cut into strips, ears and all, and dried. The stalks are tender and full of sugar. It is excellent for milch cows through the winter months; nothing gives such a yield of milk—it smells delicious when it is cured. "Come and see my alfalfa—I was told I could never grow it here, but I have six acres, next year I shall have twenty. It is the best green fodder for cattle, and ought to yield four crops in the year. It is sown with a nurse-crop of barley or oats, next year it will grow by itself."

We look at the alfalfa, which I recognize as Lucerne grass, it shows bravely green among the oat stubble; I wonder at the yield on this hard clay soil—and say so.

"After each crop I water the fields with liquid manure, that is how it is; I am making a very big liquid manure pit with pumps and special tanks for carrying it round; I use the peat which overlies all the unreclaimed part of the farm for litter in the stables and byres and piggery. It is a perfect deodorizer and retains the liquid manure, making a very valuable dressing."

I am astonished—this rich and fertile land looks

like anything but peat, but she points to the far distance where a wide belt of smoke hangs in the air, blotting out the horizon; for a long time I had been idly admiring its beautiful blue when it drifted against the green background of a grove of pines— inexperience having failed to grasp the activity it meant.

" There is more being reclaimed. The men are harrowing the fire into the soil, sometimes the peat is so deep that all the winter snows do not put it out; it smoulders, it never flames—come and see."

We walk on and on, and presently I see a wonderful picture. Up against pines and sky is the blue-white smoke, half hidden in it is a team of bay horses, through it comes the guiding cry of the man who drives without a whip, beyond is barren land if one could only see it, back where we have come lie the rich fields hot with the August sun, in the distance is the dark irregular line of the Laurentian Mountains. My companion speaks almost passionately, " It is an indescribable joy, this turning of the wild into fertile plains,—I can never have enough of it,—I do not grudge one second of the work, hard and exacting as it is,—I am repaid a thousandfold when my days and weeks of anxious care are borne into blossom like this. When the peat is burned out, the soil has to be drained, after which there is none more productive; in two years I have tile-drained forty acres and reclaimed forty-five or fifty as well." . . .

She talks eagerly, too fast for me to remember half; chiefly I gather the knowledge that she is wholly happy in her life, warm and proud in its promise and results. I carry in my mind the picture of that cultured woman, transplanted from the hectic life of Paris and London to this healthy, busy land, and my heart sings with praise of her and love of her courage.

We walk back, past buckwheat just off bloom; past a heavy crop of oats in shock with a fine catch of clover underneath, past fields of aftermath richer than many a first crop in the old country, past celery, asparagus and melon-patch to the chicken-runs and bee-butts. Looking at these last, standing near thirty acres of clover in bloom, I know where came the fragrant honey which has already pleased me so much—I only know one kind with a better flavour, and that is the heather honey near Dartmoor in Devonshire. The chickens are pure-bred, of different strains, and, in fact, I found my hostess was as particular about her stock as about her fields; a herd of splendid cows come lowing out of the byre as we approach, thoroughbred Ayrshires, with some crossed Jersey for dairy purposes. Inside we find the bull, a sturdy rascal, long and flat of back, short in the legs, a fine Ayrshire. He suffers my admiration with perfect unconcern, and we pass on to look at the silo, and the bins of food.

"Here are the scales—I have all the food in winter weighed and noted. I know how much each cow eats and the cost of it; her daily yield of milk is weighed and tested every ten days to find the amount of butter-fat to every pound of milk she gives, every cow is numbered, and each one that proves unlucrative is weeded out and a new selection made in her place." We got into the dairy, a model of cleanliness and thrifty management—but I strike at the "root" fields and am too tired to even look at the piggeries, though I love pigs. Truth to tell, I am a little dazed, and I want to go indoors and write away my bewilderment.

In my imagination swim two pictures, harrying me with positive discomfort. I see all the clever, good-looking women I know in London, scores of them, wearing their futile lives away on the social treadmill while here is such a life to be led in such a country. What one woman has done others may do. I wonder why they lack courage? It is a

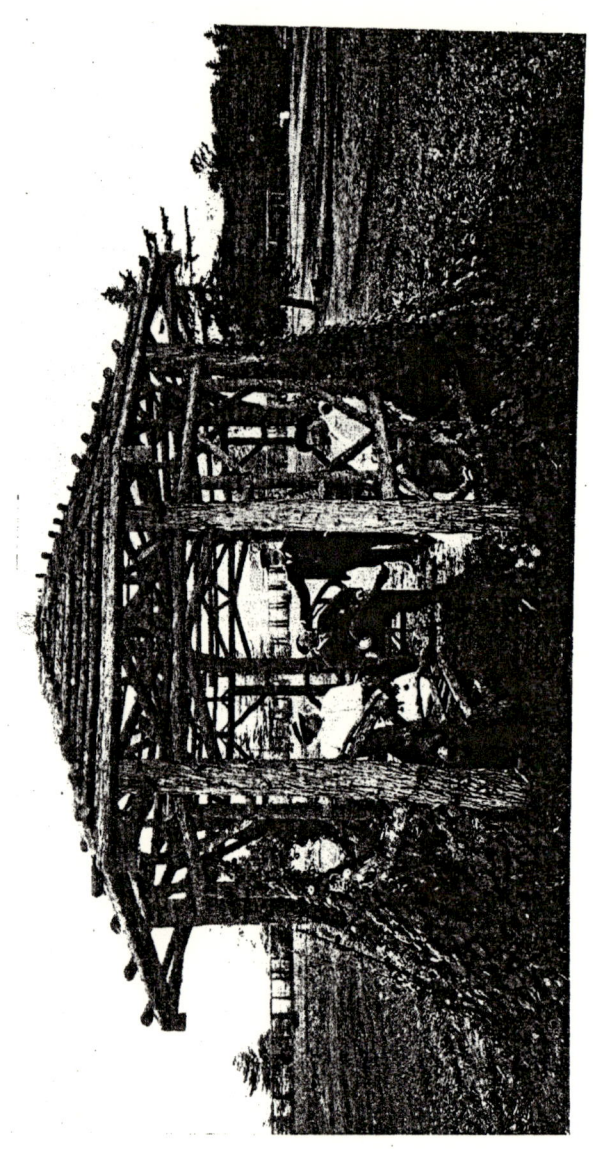

wonder, not quite new-born, but growing stronger with everything I see.

Caledonia Springs fills me with enthusiasm for farming, and I go next to Ottawa to see the head of the Experimental Farms, and learn what help the Dominion Government extends to its settling farmers. And when I reach Ottawa what a charming city it is; beautifully spaced, built like a garden city on the banks of two rivers, with fair streets, well kept, linked by an excellent tram service. Hanging over all the pretty houses, with their verandahs and lawns, are the quaint, primitive telegraph poles, leaning drunkenly in every direction, filling the alien heart with apprehension lest they fall and devour the passer-by. Rockliffe Park, which towers along the edge of the Ottawa River, is a splendid public way, romantic and discreetly wild. An air of the same picturesque savagery lurks in the names, about the beautiful city, the Rideau Falls like a curtain of pale water, the Chaudière, the boiling kettle, Lake Deschênes, edged with thick woods, the lake of pines.

I wander about the town and like it. I like the lawns round every house, that lie open and airy to the pavement edge, unfenced, unhedged. I like the perspective of roofs, "tiled" with painted wooden shingles, and oddly barren to a London eye of chimney pots. I like the hospitable hearths that offer me courteous welcome. I feel I am in a land of distinctive character, not one which apes a civilization it cannot yet afford; it has the dignity of hard-won prosperity, and than that there is no greater in the world. I am taken to see the Exhibition by earnest friends, who strive in every way to rub the gloss off my English ignorance of Canada and its resources, till I grow so weary with admiring that we leave the vegetables, poultry, pigs and the rest and walk back in the cool evening by the Driveway, the most charming feature of Ottawa; it is one of the things which I shall remember best when I return to grey London, with its perspective of young trees turning red and yellow, as I have seen it so often in the evening before the stars had driven away the sunset. I shall remember it because the first night I arrived I sat out on the verandah of my hostess's pretty house, and looked over the Driveway to the shining water wondering at the beauty of everything. It all seemed so serene and nobly planned, so like a garden that played at being a city, under the glamour of the sunset. That first admiration has proved to be one of the few things in life I am permitted to retain unspoiled; neither

daylight nor sunset, moonlight nor starlight has made me lose or modify my first keen pleasure in beautiful Ottawa.

I never appreciated the vastness of Canada until I went to inspect the Experimental Farm at Ottawa. Then I realized, almost with violence, the great area of our colony, for here was a very large farm run with an expensive staff for purely experimental reasons; an enterprise which must involve a considerable yearly outlay, which yet is continually justified by the excellence of its work and the certainty of its usefulness. The farm at the official capital is the head farm of the system, the under farms scattered about the Dominion are demonstrative rather than tutelary. The Government supports nine of them altogether, for besides this one there is one in Nova Scotia for the three maritime provinces, two in Saskatchewan, two in Alberta, one in Manitoba, one in British Columbia, and one at Lethbridge for irrigation and dry farming experiments. Here the farmers send their problems and difficulties; here the anxious settler sends his drinking water for analysis; here the resources of the country are weighed, considered and reported upon by skilled experts. I am taken through one or two departments in detail, and learn in this way some of the work done by the farm. A very interesting hour was that I spent in the company of Dr. Charles Saunders, who is the cereal expert; he is at present working to discover the best grain for the west provinces. There are new sections of the country continually being opened up which are not thoroughly understood, for these he breeds and tests grains untiringly. So much of the prosperity of Canada depends on her grain export that it is of the first importance that the highest standard be maintained. The price of wheat in Canada is the price of wheat in Liverpool, less the cost of getting it there, and the best quality only must find its way to Liverpool unless prices are to drop. "Dr. Charles" has his own flour-mill on the farm, and when he has bred a new variety of wheat he proceeds to grind and bake it, so that he may be sure of its goodness or badness from every point of view. The patience needed for his work is extraordinary; it takes from three to six years to establish a type, provided he does not observe more than half-a-dozen different characters. From the baker's point of view the best wheat is that which possesses the power to make a big loaf, chiefly consisting of air, a large percentage of water, and very little flour. To combine these excellent qualities with a wheat as near as possible to the "Red Fife," which is the standard wheat, but one which will ripen earlier is what " Dr. Charles " is now trying for. In barley the principal problem is to get stiff straw, and in oats to get one that will thrash out clean from the hull. In fact, he is aiming at getting hull-less oats. When a new type is secured that promises well, small bags of the grain for seeding purposes are sent out free of charge to the farmers. Some of the best results have been obtained from crosses with the wheat from India.

From the austere man who melts into enthusiasm directly he touches his grain specimens I am taken to see Dr. Fletcher, the entomologist, and the vital importance of his branch of work in a fruit and corn growing country even my urban intelligence can detect. Here battle is waged against parasites, blight, locusts, and every imagined insect or grub which destroys or harms useful products. Like his fellow-workers, Dr. Fletcher is heart and soul in his work. " Here," he says, "is a most useful beast; this is the parasite of the wheat aphis, which is the great plague of wheat; the food supply is too irregular for us to cultivate it, as fortunately the wheat aphis does not appear every season, but the knowledge of this parasite is a valuable factor in allaying anxiety. A farmer distracted with fear sent us samples of grain the other day which were obviously infected with dreaded plague. On close examination we found our friend and ally, the parasite, also in possession, and we were able to assure him his crop was perfectly safe." As he talks the Doctor shows me creature after creature of every degree of grub hideousness, from the pink-horned·ash-tree sphinx to the loathsome vineyard caterpillar. "It is our business," he explains, "to become aware of the time of danger to each crop from each grub." [1]

I leave him looking at his lunar moths, absorbed and content. I think the happiest men and women in the world are the workers who love their work.

Dr. Saunders, senior, is waiting for me, dressed all in furs like a woolly bear, with humorous, gentle eyes. He is taking me to the apple-house, and tells me on the way that his cross apples are increasing in size. He is trying to breed out an apple that will stand the north-western cold. It is being tried with a cross of the hardy little crab-apple variety, and results are promising well. One variety, indeed, grew double as big this year, which is highly satis-factory; he tells me too that one or two trees lived

[1] Since that visit Dr. Fletcher has died. The work of this famous entomologist has been of inestimable value to Canada.

through the winter at Indian Head, and he will have them grafted on stock and tested as soon as possible. We arrive at the apple-house, and I spend half-an-hour learning names and habits of countless fine established varieties of Canadian apples. "Winter Rose," with its mauve bloom; ".Winter St. Lawrence," streaked like a Provence rose; "Fameuse," a little dry but a good traveller, and one—a dream of all good in an apple—red and shiny, white of flesh, embarrassingly juicy, with a fine aroma and full, rich flavour. I ask its name and learn it is the "Red Mackintosh." I shall always think of that apple as the ideal.

Then we pass on to glance at the big Clydes and the grades with Percheron blood in them, they have just come into the stables and each teamster is grooming his own team. We pass into Babel and out again after a glimpse at the stout hogs. During twelve or fourteen years the farm has bred up the length of body in swine *above* the standard, and now they sell one hundred and fifty to two hundred pigs a year for breeding only. The "Improved Large Yorkshire" are the hardiest and best liked, though from a purely æsthetic point of view I confess to a preference for the chubby Berkshires and tawny Tamworths. In the byre I learn a new thing. I thought I knew every breed of cattle in the British Empire, but here is one I never heard of, the "Canadians." They are a distinct variety, bred from the Normandy cattle, imported by the first settlers two hundred years ago. There is a look of Jersey in the black muzzles and points, but they are bigger and darker; there is a good deal of red in their tone; here and there, but seldom, a patch of grey-white; they are hardy and have a heavy coat. They are bigger than the Ayrshires, yielding milk of the Ayrshire type, but richer and greater in quantity. Unlike the Ayrshires they are built on the dairy model. Herds of pure Ayrshires and Guernseys make the byre a deeply interesting department. I learn of the experiments in feed conducted to discover which gives the greatest yield of milk; experiments of feed on the steers to discover the quickest and most profitable methods of fattening. Dr. Saunders drives me round the arboretum where experiments are conducted on the growth, habit and use of trees and where hedges are grown in every sort of material; they are wanted for windbreaks in the West. And so it is in every department, the experts are engaged in solving the riddles of the settlers, in making it easy to obtain the best results from the land, and the farmers receive all the benefits of the experimental farms free of charge. I leave, deeply conscious that in such men and such work lie the real strength and the great future of Canada. In this tireless research is hidden rewards beyond the dreams of noisy oratory or bubble fame; rewards which descend on children's children and benefit nations. The agricultural education of Canada is a thing to rejoice in—the Dominion Government has webbed its people in a vast collegiate system. It begins with the rural schools, dictated by the eminent educationalist Professor James Robertson. He set it forth that "any system of education which aims at, or proposes to help the people who work on the farms, must be a system that will help the elementary schools, where the future men and women of the farm will get their formal education."

The rural schools are fast giving place to the consolidated schools, where agriculture is a prominent study. To supply qualified teachers for this reform in education, Sir William MacDonald provided the Ontario Agricultural College at Guelph with two institutions for the special purpose of educating teachers. In nearly every province is to be found a large Agricultural College of which the one at Guelph is the chief. The Farmers' Institute and the Experimental Farms just described will give help in the vast network of agricultural education which overspreads Canada.

The same day that I see the Experimental Farm my friends, zealous for my education, take me from the farm to a great timber-yard, but only a haze of impressions is left on a brain already worn with wonder! It is a visit to be taken seriously, for timber has made much of the wealth in Canada. First, we go through a paper factory, where wood is made into paper, and we acquire a fogged picture of whirling wheels and relentless energy, of sawdust, pulp, and noise—incoherent, but very impressive. From that into the timber-yard is like going from the hot room to the hottest in a Turkish bath. Here a demoniacal energy and intelligence possesses everything. The tree-trunks, rushing down the water-slides, toil through a succession of frantic toilettes, which finally leave of them only sawdust, match-wood or planks. We stand, fascinated, watching iron hands of fiendish cunning seize the great trees, and arrange them before the terrible whirling blades that wait to devour; we see the trolley holding the tree pass up and down before the saw, and with every run a plank is cut as easily and neatly as if it were bread.

Big saws, little saws, in fact, all kinds of saws there are; all whirling, all noisy, all ready to devour the men who work them as readily as the sweet-smelling wood, which will never bear green leaves again or grow towards the sun. Sick and dizzy with the clatter, we pass over to the Chaudière Falls, which appear as a very Niagara to an English eye; a chaos of wild waters pouring eternally over the rocks, and making a picturesque landmark for visitors to Parliament Hill. We stand upon a wet, worn plank that sways unpleasantly beneath the feet, and get headaches with the noise of the Falls and the nervous excitement of all we have seen in the lumber-yard.

Beyond the city rise the Laurentian Mountains. They are pointed out on the way back, silhouetted against an amethyst sky. I, for one, look at them with interest. I am going to them, to stay in a little wooden house, with a butter-nut tree near by, where the blue-birds build in spring. I shall stand among the pines and hear the cow-bells ring when the cattle come down the valley at milking-time. I look, a little wistfully; cities are good, but green aisles are better, and silence best of all.

CHAPTER III

THERE are little pink clouds round the moon, which is as yet only a silver rim. On either side of the rough road stretches rich land, heavy with corn and pasture. We are riding into the West. Up against the crimson sky rises the bold outline of King's Mountain : that is where I am going, for a week among the cedars and the pines.

I am looking forward to these next few days with unfeigned joy, for they are to be spent with people whom I know, in their country home; out of the frigidities of officialdom into the warm heart of friends. I must pause here and now to explain away a carping sound in that phrase "frigidities of official-dom," for there never were in all the world kinder officials than those over here. Wherever I go I am met with leniency, with abundant courtesy, with a concentrated essence of attention. Only all the officials of all time cannot offer, with all their welcomes pressed together, one tithe of the joy

to be gathered from the clasp of the hand of a friend.

The road is very rough; where it is not inches deep in dust it is jagged with rocky stones bedded in the earth; or, more treacherous still, lying loose. We ride on a cautious rein; where we can find a stretch of grass we canter, and the horses sniff greedily at the piney wind.

We pass a tiny log-cabin : it looks old and battered. All round it is land that bears signs of arduous toil well rewarded; the very fences are made of tree-roots, beyond the ploughed land the bush grows thick. The farmers who ride with me rein up and point, saying, " There is the log hut of a settler." I look, deeply stirred.

Here came a brave man into the virgin woods; here is the very cabin he built with infinite labour of trees he himself cut down; the interstices of it he caulked with moss or oakum, and then caked with mud to stand the weather. The tiny garden is the first clearing he made, and this fruitful land round his rough homestead is the kingdom he has carved himself. The broad fields that shine so fair under the westering sun were once thick bush; every inch has been won by earnest labour; each great root in the fence of roots means an achievement of worth, for after the trees are felled there are the roots to be taken out before the land can be ploughed, a very troublesome job. I wonder if some loved woman came with him to his work; if she helped him gladly, and felt with him the primal joy of good land earned by toil. I wonder if she stood with him and watched the oats and corn come to harvest, and if they had children who were happy in their heritage. Or I wonder if he worked alone without a mate!

I turn and glance furtively at my companions; they ride straight on, the little log hut does not rouse them to any great interest. It spells work and reward—all life here spells that, and they take both for granted. The tiller of the soil owns the soil, and the harder he works the better he is repaid. The blood of pioneers runs in the veins of these men, and they would not understand if I told them how some savage instinct in me thrills and is pleased with the order of their lives. I remember the squalor, disease and alcoholism of English cities, and I look at these narrow-minded, broad-chested, hard-working men with unstinted respect. Not entire admiration, I admit, for the cultured brain is yet to come— the love of beauty in all its forms lies dormant. When they find time to tend their brains as well as

54

they do their farms and factories, they will make a splendid race.

The road winds on; now we begin to climb out of the valley; a scarlet tanager flies across our path like a patch of the sunset; the air, which has vibrated all day with the cry of grasshoppers, grows momentarily still. Very soon the crickets and frogs will sing evensong, but for a little space there seems a lull. The light is growing quickly less; there are no twilights to speak of at this time of year; night descends like a drop-scene and hides the beautiful stage of the world. A cat-bird mews from the bush; the sumac-trees, with their chocolate plumes grown eerily black, look like sentinel hearses; the Michaelmas daisies, which have hung their pale purple mist beside our path all the time, begin to glower, ghostly wan; the evening primrose distils fine essences; our horses sniff the end of their journey and toss their heads. We pass a wayfarer; he is lighting the lantern which will be his only street-lamp; we are on the mountain road, away on our right twinkle a few lights. A star glitters ahead of us; it grows bigger; it is a star bowered in trees. The farmers, in whose care I have ridden, point to it: "There is the house."

A few more moments and I am at a wooden house, built on piles among maple-trees. A happy voice breaks upon my ears : "We thought you were never coming." I pass through the wire-netting doors to a wonderful supper of fruit, corn-cakes and maple syrup; then I sleep gloriously in the mountain air.

It is hard to understand how people suffer starvation in England when there is this great Colony crying for clever, industrious workers. We walk out in the bright morning sunshine, and wild raspberries are brushed to the earth by our skirts as we pass, the crab-apple tree is bowed down with its load of fruit; the beech-nuts and the butter-nut trees give proof of their plenty in the chattering of squirrel and chipmunk; the stone we stumble over is a beautiful green-and-pink thing of crystals; it is phosphate—invaluable for manure; near it lies a little sheet of yellow glass. I pick it up. "It looks like the talc they face some of the motor veils with in the old country," I muse. "It is mica," answers my pretty hostess; "there seems to be a vein of it wherever that pink rock lies. The ground is full of it."

One day we go to the top of King's Mountain, and look across the Ottawa River to the miles of cornland and pasture, wrested from luxuriant bush which gives such a pleasing aspect to Canadian scenery. Away on our left the Parliament Buildings brood over the capital city. We can dimly see them through a blue haze of smoke; there on the flank of the mountain lies a pretty mere, shaped like a tennis racket, and dotted with boats and boat-houses. On the way down we meet a young man and woman of such typical beauty that I am roused to interest. She is a supple, well-built creature, with red-brown hair drawn demurely back Pompadour-wise from her brow; her eyes are gentle and set far apart; her mouth is compassionate; the man beside her is tall and slim, with the long, dark face and stormy eyes which go in this country with a trace of Indian blood. He is extraordinarily handsome; they make a very pleasant pair. They walk up the long green aisle of trees, and the girl carries a large bunch of maidenhair and wild orchids, which she had gathered on the way up the mountain. " They look like a bridal pair coming to some primeval altar," I say. " Are they betrothed?" My hostess looks at them kindly. " No, poor children, they would like to be, but her people will not permit it, as he is a Roman Catholic." I am saddened by this glimpse of strong cross-currents in the seeming even flow of the country life; and I realize again with force how powerful is the French-Canadian element. The shores of the Ottawa River beyond Lake Deschênes are lined with rich homesteads, owned by Macdonalds and Macgregors and every kind of Mac, who are all Roman Catholics, and only speak French!

Such a housewife as Nan is, to be sure! "A place for everything, and everything in its place" is never spoken, but always practised. After a day or two I myself develop strange leanings to order, and am pleased beyond expression to find a match with its head off under the upturned glass on my wash-stand. I tidy it up neatly, wondering at Meg; I remember having spied it before and leaving it for Meg or Aunt Phœbe to spread their passionate tidiness upon. At lunch I am swept by a domestic monsoon.

" Phœbe dear, you must have dusted it off."

" I don't think so, my dear, no, I don't think so."

Meg looks at slim little old Phœbe with pity. The quavering voice repeats denial. Such a musical old voice, sweet and tremulous; it belongs to the ivory face and beautiful hair. I will not mind being old if I can have such soft white hair, all garnered into a silken knob.

" No, I saw it and left it. I am sure I did. But my memory is going. I don't think I dusted it off."

" It " proves to be the match. A housewifely device of Nan's to drain the tooth-glass dry. I

behead another and put it back under the rim of my glass, full of a remorseful knowledge that any attempt to tidy in this household is painting the lily, perfuming the rose.

They work unostentatiously but ceaselessly, these two dear women, at the daily grind of cooking, washing up, dusting, sweeping. Servants are hard to get in Canada, and when found very expensive, ill-trained and independent. Every clever good-looking woman who comes over marries almost at once. The wives of Canada seem to take it for granted that they shall be mistress and servant in one, and very excellently they do their work. The days wear by in peaceful, happy dreaming. I sit beneath the maple-tree where cat-birds mew and squirrels flash from bough to bough, trying to unravel a tangle of notes and plan a more definite method of record for the rest of my journey. Meg and Phœbe slip noiselessly about the house, and at eventide, with a great hubbub of rejoicing, we go along the road to meet Gaston, who comes in every day from his office. "Has he brought the can of maple syrup," we wonder, "and has he a letter from Guy"—the singer son beloved and only, in New York.

After dinner we all wander round the moor looking at the blue of the juniper bushes, laughing when

we pass the little marsh where I was to be taken to
see the flags blooming if I were not satisfied with
the flowers in Canada! There are no flags now,
those are all over, but the frogs croon pleasantly, and
a wealth of later flowers ridicules my old complaint.
We wander away into the bush and look at a neigh-
bouring farmer's mica mine; he has probably found
a fortune on his land, the land he has been tilling,
and his fathers before him, content to make a modest
livelihood. He is not at all hysterical about the
discovered ore; he works it, with his sons to help, in
odd hours, and not on an extensive scale. In between the work necessary to keep the established farm
in good working order they blast away the pink stone,
and take out the shining layers of crackling stuff.
Even working so, at such comparatively trifling cost
of time, they took out a load last week which sold for
1700 dollars (£340). It is a sane and sensible way
to make the most of the property. If the mica fails
there is the farm, but if the vein is as rich as it
promises there will be the accumulated money gained
by this slow work to finance bigger operations by
and by. We stand at the edge of the pit and look
down at its glistening sides. There is great silence
in the bush, no one is at work here to-day; Gaston
is in his happy hunting mood, and chatters delight-

fully of his adventures with moose and caribou. While I listen I handle his gun with reverence; he has it for sure—it is early, but bears have been known to come down earlier from the mountains. As we go back through the sudden dusk with Aunt Phœbe flitting like a pale night moth before us, I wonder how I can ever tell in whatsoever words the beauty of this lovely country, the romantic simplicity of its life.

There is a little sadness in my wondering. To-morrow is Saturday, and on Monday I take the west-ward track of my journey. I hate to leave, and tell them so. Gaston cheers me up by saying Saturday is a holiday, so he will not go into the city to-morrow, and promising to take me for a walk.

"To-morrow." Gaston is in his tiresome mood, or at least Meg says he is. He wanders about the kitchen talking politics, and she says they are no relation to jam. I am trying to write on the verandah; the "Conditions of Canada from a Woman's Point of View" mingle with the sounds that creep through the wire-netted door. Gaston is dogmatizing about the "communal assets," whatever they are, and Meg is punctuating his theories with "two lbs."—"three lbs."—"how many pounds will three times three-quarters make?" As his voice sinks into a judicial drone I hear her declare in exasperation that she has forgotten how much sugar is already in the pot. A thrill of sympathy urges me into the fray.

"Take me for that walk, Gaston," I beg. "Let us see if Dandy's apples are fit to pick!"

We leave Meg troubled, like Martha, about many things, and start forth on the mountain road. With our faces to the sunset he forgets politics and talks delightfully about golden orioles, scarlet tanagers, cherry-birds and brown threshers—never was such an observer of the quiet, sweet ways of Nature, never was a man less inclined to speak of what he knows. We dawdle along, stopping now and then to "pop" the seed-vessels of the wild orchids, or coax a squirrel to chatter from his leafy porch. We are going to admire Dandy's orchard, the best in the country-side, I am told, and when I see it I can well believe it—an apple-orchard in the spring is a lovely sight indeed, but it has its merits in the autumn. As we draw near Jack spies a tuft of hair in a barbed wire fence, and thereupon sets up such a frantic whimpering that his master guesses he has smelt bear.

"It must be pretty fresh," he adds, watching the antics of the dog, who is sniffing round in circles and finally races up the road. We examine the tuft, and he says it's bear all right.

"I promised to send two wire-haired fox terriers to Otto the guide at Leanchoil," I say, brooding over the scraggy hair. "That's the place for sport! I can't think why people don't come out to Canada every year and get real shooting, instead of hiring a moor and playing at it in Scotland. Otto wants big dogs; he is going to train them for bear-tracking—I don't know if I shall find him what he wants."

Gaston snorts disapproval.

"We would be much wiser to get beagles like Jack. He is the kind for bear!"

My respect for the little busybody yapping in the far distance goes up with a leap.

"What's his measure?" I ask.

"He's fifteen inches; too big for show, but splendid for work. He has no——"

Suddenly Gaston falls on hands and knees, and grovels ecstatically over the soft mud.

"By Jove! he's a big fellow. Look here."

I also grovel, and suffer an indescribable thrill at the sight of the big fresh spoor. For the first time in my life I am close to bear; the mark is exactly like the sketches that wander about the margins of Seton-Thompson's book in my library in London. I would know it anywhere—the flat heel, the break, the spread claws further on. We measure with a stick, and Gaston says it's a good ten inches. We notch the stick to verify the measurement later, and I listen with all the reverence of green inexperience while Gaston begins Sherlock-Holmesy descriptions of the doings of the bear within the last few hours. His keen eyes are shining, his interest is so keenly centred on the spoor that when Dandy hails us from the orchard, our goal for so long, he starts like a frightened child!

"Here, you!" says the voice, "come and help drive. Have you a gun, Gaston? The dog is on the track of that big fellow."

Gaston starts at a run—so do I—up the road, into the orchard, with the grasshoppers flying tempestuously before our feet, crushing sweet odours from juniper and wild asters in our way; Dandy has his ˙303, and is full of sympathy when he sees our empty hands. He offers it to Gaston, who magnanimously says he will beat, babbling tales of the damage his orchard has lately sustained from the big fellow. We try to get another gun, but only find a single shot ˙22 which Gaston sniffs at, but which I thankfully carry in a pathetic belief that even a pop-gun were better than nothing. Away in the bush Jack is giving tongue, and his deep note is so like the familiar sound of an English foxhound that I have a mental picture of a harried bear scudding across country with a pack of one beagle scudding in the rear, and ourselves, a field of three, scudding a long way behind. A ridiculous picture. It jostles in my imagination as I run beside Dandy, and I feel I would hardly be surprised to see the bush open out, to find this heavy going yield to the satin smoothness of Doctor's stride over the heather and furze and bracken of far-away Devonshire! We are nearing the sound—suddenly I realize that this moment means neither heather nor fox, but bush and bear. . . . I look at Dandy; he is quite happy, peering earnestly in every direction, and listening attentively; Jack is kicking up a fearful fuss somewhere close—I stare in the direction of the sound, and am all at once unceremoniously tugged to the ground.

"Hide! Quick!"

We crouch behind a shrub—Dandy examines his gun, and I curse the nasty feeling, like toothache, which pervades the hiatus between ribs and hips.

"See where he is?" says my companion. Cautiously I look ahead. There is a big black bear shambling away; Jack, in a state of violent excitement, is making occasional darts at his quarters; every now and then the bear stands up and lays back his little ears, inviting the enemy to "come on" with a snarling growl and an ugly display of teeth. As

E 65

he gets away we come out of hiding and follow on. I begin to realize the plan of campaign; Gaston has gone round to head the bear back to us—and Jack's importance in the game is great. The gallant little chap knows perfectly well what he is about, harrying and delaying the big brute, whose one idea is to shake off this tiresome pestilence at his heels and retire up the mountain to digest his stolen apples. With a marvellous regard for opportunity and distance, Jack snaps again and again between knee and heel, leaping back three or four feet to safety after each bite; my blood warms with admiration—this is the kind of dog for Otto the guide at Leanchoil! Suddenly we duck again behind a bush. The bear is coming our way, he has seen Gaston. Dandy takes the little ·22 from me roughly and presses his gun into my scared hands.

"Wait till he gets to the clear place and rears— then shoot straight—take a fine sight."

The burly mass crushing towards us through the undergrowth swims for a second in a haze of terror— then he rears; mechanically I aim, mechanically fire —and then push the gun back to Dandy. The bear tosses his head as though he had been flicked in the face by a whip, and then puts it down to the ground and turns a complete somersault, just as I have seen

his performing brothers do in circuses. For one swelling instant I fancy I have killed him—then he comes straight for us, swift and wicked. At his heels is Jack the indefatigable. In frank terror I turn to flee—he rears again, bleeding and furious. A ping and a thud—the soft welcome thud of stricken flesh —and he kneels over slowly, grudgingly. Dandy, the wary old hunter, cool and deadly steady, has given him the straight shot.

Gaston comes up and tells his adventures over the corpse, then we tell ours, Dandy politely offering me the skin, which I refuse with a heartache—I know very well I have not earned it—I neither found, nor drove, nor killed him. Besides, it is a very poor skin. By and by we drag him head foremost to the edge of the bush (not a light task, as he must weigh 300 lbs.), and there we leave him for Dandy to fetch with a horse and cart.

The sun is sinking behind the mountain as we turn towards home; Jack trots after us with wagging tail and weary lolling tongue. As we draw near we see Meg smiling on the verandah, and in the lighted kitchen behind her stand pots of jam in rows and rows to cool.

*   *   *   *   *   *

I was talking about Gaston's bear to some one on

the tram one day, and he said he had heard a much
finer bear story from a friend in British Columbia—
which I privately thought very possible—and he
said his friend's letter was worth having. He sent
me a copy, and I reproduce it. Here, then, are two
bear stories, one in English fashion, one in trans-
atlantic—

"Well, Mac, the white ducks are quite plentiful
at present, we have four for dinner; the geese and
mallards are all gone. The clams are quite plentiful
too, so you see we are living on the best. But what
I want to tell you is that you are not a judge of *swift
bears* any more. Alfred and I killed one the other
day that was so *swift* that high velocity is a slow
word compared to that bear. I think this one is a
new breed that you never studied about.

"You see the kid and I were out gathering a few
white fellows at the head, and managed to get a few,
when the kid spied Mr. Bear, and said, 'See the
little bear?' so we rowed up to the shore, and brave
as a lamb I gets out of the boat and walks up to
Mr. Bruin and lets him have it a couple of times in
the face; it was then that he realized that something
was going to be doing, it did not take long either.

"Well, he started in my direction, and I had the
same idea as he had, and I started in the same direc-

tion (no chance for an argument), but I was a little ahead, and when I started I was on the level, so I had no trouble in keeping the lead, because every time I'd look back he was just crawling out of one of the tracks I made, and that would give me a chance to shoot again and go on (brave boy). When we got pretty close to the water with the race, the kid saw things were getting interesting for yours truly, and thought he'd make a flank movement on the enemy; so on he came with the (hoolet) run and ˙22 rifle in hand, and took deliberate aim and potted Mr. Bear square in the eye and knocked it out (good shot, eh !).

"Well, the bear could only see on one side, and he started to circle (this is where the speed is); when he commenced to go around we could see one bear, after a while two bears appeared, then three bears, and after a while they looked like one big long bear.

"Well, at first when he began to circle it was quite a job to hit him because we had to shoot at the single bear.

"But after he looked like one long bear all we had to do was to shoot at the circle, and the shot that missed him on the near side he was always surely around on time to catch it on the other (you see, I was using the shot-gun and fine shot). Sometimes he had to side-step to keep from running himself down.

"Well, after he ran for a while the circle had a gap in it that showed the weight of shot was beginning to tell, because we certainly poured it into him; and when he died we were unable to take him home that night, so the next morning the three of us went after him, and were just able to move him, and thought that too much work and left him; and when the tide came in we took the gasoline launch *Queen* up and run her nose in the mud and hitched the little anchor chain on him, which was plenty strong enough, and then we started the gypsy to work and hauled him in and took him out to deep water. Then to skin him we were going to hang him on one of the davits, but when the weight came on the boat she listed till the guard-rail dipped water.

"Well, to take the hide off the son-of-a-gun we had to use a cold chisel and tin shears on account of so much lead in him. He's nice and tender to eat, but all the meat has got to be fried to get the lead melted out of it, and at one frying of meat enough lead is melted to make a jig-hook (you wouldn't have to burn your fingers now melting lead).

"He was very fat, but the fat is very heavy on the stomach because there is so much lead mixed in it.

"Alfred has grown so much since he made the famous shot that the other day he was going to take a swim, but couldn't find deep enough water in Port Neville Harbour to float him.

"Well, Mac, if I were to tell anybody else about that bear they'd *think* I was lying, but you know me too well to even stop to *think*.

"I'll tell you more about the bear when I come home; give me more time to think.

"Your old, etc."

* * * * * *

I like that bear story.

CHAPTER IV

FISHING ON STEEL RIVER

I AM trying to do two things at once, and doing neither well. One eye is fixed on the end of the avenue watching for " Jimmy's " cart to appear, and the other is entertained with the impudence of a chipmunk which is gambolling at my very feet, having made up his mind, after a good deal of soul-searching, that I am a harmless by-product of literature, and in no way designed for his discomfiture. My host and hostess are down at the well; last week they had it cleaned, and in the process traces of copper and mica were discovered; every day, since then, they have made a pilgrimage to the well, hunting among the *débris* for fair-sized samples to be sent away for analysis. I know what they are saying, though I cannot hear them—dear things ! He is telling her of the good time he will give her if they find ore in their land, and she is saying he *could* not give her a better one if they had a million dollars a minute. They have been married twenty-seven years, and still have the hearts of children. The cat-bird mews on from the maple overhead, down the valley the cow-bells tinkle—the world glows so still and fair in this dewy morning-tide that if it were not selfish I could wish they would find no mica, and live their Arcadian life for ever in this happy little wooden house on the mountains. But the soil is full of phosphates—they may easily find their mica; Canada is teeming with undiscovered riches, and the romances of sudden wealth are very common.

I see the pair-horse rig coming, heralded by a vast column of dust; there has been no rain for two weeks, and very little before that, so the heavens and earth and very brooks seem to have turned to dust. The chipmunk scuttles frantically into his underground nest, the geologists rush up from the well, and I kiss them with fervent good-bye. I scramble into the seat with luggage like a barricade around me, and set forth in the pillar of dust for Ottawa. I am going to catch the midday western train, and I am curious both as to the pleasures or otherwise of a long train journey in this country. We arrive at the Central Station far too early, and I spend the best part of a very hot hour studying a poster issued by the Canadian Pacific Railway offering special rates to harvesters, and stating that 25,000 are needed on the western wheatfields. Yet I know perfectly well that next winter in the London dailies will be raised the usual "Emigrant's Bitter Cry," engineered by the trade-unionists to keep men from coming out and making labour cheaper. We shall read of the destitution and suffering of Englishmen in Canadian cities who have been lured out by big promises and failed to get work on landing; we shall be told of this starving case and that starving case, but not of the existence of this poster, nor of the high wages men can earn who are willing to work on the land.

The English emigrant seems to be generally an urban, and it appears to me that the worker in cities for the needs of cities is *likely* to be idle in a land where cities hardly exist. If the skilled worker in cities goes out to a land of few and small cities, prepared to dig trenches in the streets rather than turn himself back to the soil, the mother of health and giver of wealth, he has small right to a hearing when he utters his "bitter cry." The point should be not to ventilate the failure of the unfitted who have gone to a new country and refused to adapt themselves to its needs (though that is deplorable enough), but to insist widely and tirelessly on the kind of immigrant likely to succeed in Canada. Here is this magnificent colony of ours, this land of wood and water, mountain and plain, crying for hands to gather the wealth from its thousands of miles of fruit-bearing, ore-bearing, wheat-bearing, lumber-bearing soil, and here are the few hundreds of town-bred and trained men who, when they are put on the farms, will not stay there, raising the " Emigrant's Bitter Cry." It gives one to weep! It affects the mental attitude of the Canadians to the mother country; they are beginning to judge of England by the men she sends out who "will not stay on the farms."

I have succeeded in growing very interested in the whole social problem that surges between this green poster and the "hunger-marchers" I saw just before I left England, in Surrey *en route* for London—interested in the problems of the noise and fuss they raise in the demand for work, and the scorn—the bitter, hideous scorn—with which they are regarded as workers here when they do come out—when the clang of a great bell tells me the Winnipeg train is coming, and I hurry off to " check " my baggage. Canada is far ahead of us in luggage arrangements, and behind us in her telegraph system; but I am wandering. There is so much to say about everything that I keep forgetting what I meant to say when I began the chapter.

l find my " sleeper," booked two days ago because

of the press of travel, and start forth on the journey. The first day proves almost unbearable by reason of the heat and dust; the windows have to be kept shut because the dust penetrates and defiles everything; the platform at the rear of the train is quickly deserted by even the most ardent lover of air, for it is impossible to be cooled by a draught which is laden with sand and coal-cinders. But with evening comes comfort; the stifling heat abates, the green world moving past our windows begins to glow with the tender lights of a brilliant sunset which has merged into dusk—the short, quick dusk of these latitudes—overhead swings a young moon, and life renews itself in our veins. After dinner the car is transformed into a dormitory with a long green lane in the middle between the discreet curtains which give a sort of privacy to sleep. I make for my number, and am greatly perplexed at the way all books and writing materials, not to mention the necessary dressing-case, have disappeared. I find them at last stored neatly in odd corners, and then discover a big paper bag hanging by the window, taking a lot of room and nothing whatever to do with me. I hunt for the nigger conductor and deliver it back to him with offensive honesty. He is very nice about it. It contains my hat! The bags are pro-

vided by a kindly Company to save them from the ravages of dust. My sleeping berth proves luxurious, and I am rocked into instantaneous delicious slumber by the easy motion of the train.

In the morning I learn for the first time in my life the real fascination of train travelling. Rain in the night has laid all dust, a brilliant breeze scuds by, we are nearing the shores of Lake Superior, the country is wonderful in its wild beauty; here are mountains clothed in pine and cedar like Pisgah's self, here a deep ravine with a clear bright river swirling through, there a lake fringed with rushes, here a patch of meadowsweet, here a crag green with ferns, there a pool so deeply, clearly brown that one smells peat only to look at it!

Everything pleases, even the blue glass insulators on the telegraph posts are one with the landscape, though I privately entertain a great contempt for telegrams in Canada. I keep the rear platform despite the breeze which is growing chilly; we draw up at intervals and perform, I suppose, some engineering duties at such times. At one I watch the patient faces of innumerable oxen on a cattle train bound east; they seem at peace with their estate and unsuspicious of the future; at another I am entertained to see a couple of platelayers making

77

a hearty dessert on wild raspberries gathered by the track. At last a stoppage comes, when it is borne in on me that I have been looking at freight-car 10,670 for a very long time—I know its "inside length" is 32 feet 6 inches, its "inside width" is 8 feet, its "inside height" 6 feet 4 inches; I know its "capy." is 40,000 lbs., its "tare" 27,000 lbs.; I know it has 7 rungs on its iron ladder, and I know the exact shape of the little iron pocket for an address label. It strikes me we are staying a very long time at this wooden house which pretends to be the station of a township, and is really only a lonely little house in the bush where the single rail doubles for a few hundred yards. I learn in due course that there has been a freight collision ahead of us, and that we have to wait until the line is cleared—also that it may take all night. We get off and walk about, some of us climb below the track and come back laden with sunflowers and Michaelmas daisies, which make a brilliant display on the dining-tables. We are delayed ten hours over that little mishap; and I am glad indeed to hear next morning that this is Lake Superior, and we are making good time for Winnipeg. As I look at the splendid bays with big billows breaking on a rocky coast, it takes me several minutes to realize that these are the shores of an inland lake, that the dark waves curling and breaking over rocks are fresh-water waves, that all the wide expanse of white-crested water out to the far horizon is not indeed the sea. If I had happened on this scene suddenly without knowing how I got there, I would have thought I was at Bude or Penzance or Scilly, but never on the border of Lake Superior.

I am sitting by the big window watching the young moon that swings overhead when we draw up at Jack Fish—I look at her wondering if I have ever seen her so wild and shy in little trim-hedged garden England when a noisy merry party of sunburnt fishermen board the car. A young boy, a tall, white-lashed, red-headed athlete, and a burly middle-aged man with the interesting guarded face of the man of the world who has grown, despite himself, into a philosopher. They are very particular about some snow-shoes they have brought with them, and talk to the conductor about them. He examines them minutely with deep interest. Later on, when it is too dark to watch the passing landscape, the conductor asks me if I would like to hear the tale of a fishing trip, which, of course, I say I would, and thank him for troubling about me. The white-lashed athlete then comes and sits with me for an hour or so, telling me a camping tale that makes me

79

envious beyond belief. His graphic slow method! I wish I could reproduce it; and the pale light of his lashes as he sometimes lifted his eyes heavily to find if I were bored or interested. Here is his story, nearly in his own words—

"The Doctor and the Young 'un and I have been fishing Mountain Lake where Steel River flows out of the lake; we had four Indians as guides, a squaw to cook for us, two canoes—a big and a little—and five tents. The lake is deep set among the mountains, with a sort of under-radiance glowing from its waters. We were too late for more than fixing up camp when we arrived at Mountain Lake, and we sat watching the Indians make camp preparations while the Doctor gave us long dissertations on any and every variety of fly, telling us we would have been wise to bring some more Montreals, and that Red Palmers were not going to help us any. He thinks he knows a lot about flies. The air was aromatic with the perfume of balsam, for the Indians cut down young balsam saplings about fifteen feet high, and make of the flat, scented boughs mattresses more springy and comfortable than any you have ever slept on, I'll bet. I asked the Doctor what country lay beyond us, and he said no man knows. Only one man, an old French-Canadian trapper, had been known to go so far, and he had never been heard of since. We speculated as to his fate, and then Joe Eskimo, our head guide and interpreter, was called and questioned. He said the Trapper went away from Jack Fish two years ago to find the falls which tradition places away up Steel River; he was a 'very strong man, and very ignorant in all but matters of his trade, could not read or write, or even tell the time by the clock,'—this from Joe, with a ridiculous gleam of superiority in his harsh eyes.

"On the morrow, and for the four following days we fished up and down stream; we learned—the Young 'un and I—for the first time in our life, what is it to have a perfect river, perfect weather, perfect sport. We learned, too, that the Doctor was right; the purple fly was best. We landed enough speckled trout daily to feed the eight of us three times a day (it was the only meat we had), splendid fellows they were, anything from two to seven pounds. We got another variety, too, which I believe in my heart were rainbow trout, but the Doctor was very obstinate about it; he said they were steel-head salmon, and that a lot of them have been put in Lake Superior; he says he once caught two in Current River, and *he* knows. But I still think they were rainbow.

Late on the fifth day we were waiting for the Young 'un, who as usual was last to finish as he was always first to begin—I never met any one in my life so silent or so keen; I remember how the light was on his hair, and how the curious faint trouty smell floated up from the creel; the two impressions were hovering idly in my mind, jostling each other incongruously, when the Doctor turned to us sharply—

"'Say, are you game to go up Steel River to morrow?'

"We thought it over. It was in the nature of exploring, this was strange country that no man knew. When we said we would he went off to talk it over with Joe Eskimo, who was perfectly certain to agree to anything that might mean 'two fingers.' These Indians are extraordinary; they are not allowed to buy whisky, but they will work harder and longer for a single tot than your British workman will shout for work—and that is saying much. There is no limit to what you can ask of them if they see 'two fingers' at the end of the day."

I sit back in the cushioned seat wondering at the story, at the teller, at his detail, his phlegm, his assurance. The Young 'un is fidgeting, and every now and then correcting some trifling inaccuracy. They seem like men who are unused to describing and fear to mis-state. The voice drones on, level, uninspiring; I take to watching the speaker and the Young 'un, and wondering if the Doctor ever got bored on the fishing trip. It is good to have some one to speak to, however, and I am less critical than grateful, although the narrative bids fair to lack interest.

"So we broke camp next morning and began to paddle up the river, which lies, I believe, about 150 miles east of Port Arthur. There was an Indian at the bow and stern of each boat, and we were making good way when we were stopped by a long jamb about two miles up; it was a fine accumulation of years, and there was nothing for it but to portage round. The Indians do the work in portaging; they take a pack-strap across the forehead, so arranging that they carry nearly the whole weight on the neck; they will take in that way 300 to 400 lbs. apiece. We blazed a trail as we went, for the bush was virgin; only once all the way did we see second growth, where had been a bush fire. The trees were fine, mostly evergreens, spruce, hemlock, balsam, tamarack, poplar and balm of Gilead—on the river-bank in the sand was the track of countless game; the Doctor sat in judgment on us while we diagnosed the marks without help from the guides. At last he told us that the big print like that of an enlarged ox meant moose—(it is an especially easy one because a moose bends down in the fetlocks and leaves the print of his dew-claw)—having learned so much we were then able to surmise that the mark as long but narrower meant caribou, and the little one, more like a goat, meant red deer; bear, too, was there, we saw bear-marks on the trees sometimes six feet high. and we saw tracks of fox and beaver and wolves in plenty.

"'If we were on a hunting trip now,' said the Doctor, 'we would have a splendid time; but we aren't. We had better do what we came for, as there are only two guns among the lot of us.'

" I did get a shot in spite of this wisdom, but that was only by luck. After negotiating that wearisome jamb and encountering a belated mosquito in the woods, we travelled up-stream and met the finest sport of our trip. The trout were not so many, perhaps, as lower down, but beauties, so large and so game. We got out on the rocks, and the wide river gave us an easy sweep; once we stopped our work to watch the Young 'un, who had forty minutes' grand struggle with a little chap; three times he leaped a good five feet like a flexible bar of silver, and as many times he shot off forty feet or so while he held him, to our indescribable excitement, for his

84

line was getting short. It was a lesson to watch him, so slim and cool out there on the rock, playing that angry little fish—he never got excited, always kept cool."

At this panegyric I survey the Young 'un. He betrays no embarrassment. The story chants on.

"We were infinitely more elated than he when at last he brought to land a shiny, speckly, broken-hearted little three-pounder. The river winds there like the coils in a motor engine! We told each other that we would camp by the granite bluff that looked about half-a-mile off, but we went on and on, it never got nearer, and after the Doctor declared we had done ten miles and we were roused to say fifteen, the bluff was still 'a quarter of a mile' away.

"Early next morning we set off in the canoes determined to locate that rock before we started to fish—the wind blew fresh and chill in our faces; I was sitting in the big canoe just behind the bow Indian, and mounting guard over the shot-gun and rifle that made our modest equipment. As we turned a bend in the river I saw the bow's hand reach to the guns; he touched the shot-gun—his eyes were fixed ahead—and I instantly took the rifle and looked round. Quite close a big bull moose was running up the bank, evidently he had heard our

85

voices, for the Doctor, as usual, was making a lot of noise, but had been unable to fix us because the wind was blowing away from him. Some one shouted 'Get him in the head,' and I promptly shot over him, a dowdy thing to do; at the unusual sound he stopped dead, and I sent the next bullet straight. He toppled into the water, and the swift current caught him, kicking vigorously, whirling him towards our canoe; we were horribly scared, for he weighed about a thousand pounds, but he passed with six feet to spare, and sank almost at once in a deep pool. The Indians said he would not rise for two or three days, but presently Joe Eskimo shouted from the small canoe, which was behind, that they had got him—they towed him to shore, where he was skinned in due course, and the guides feasted riotously on moose-steak. The Doctor pretended he liked it better than trout, of which, to tell the truth, we were all getting a little sick, but I think I would sooner eat warm indiarubber myself. It might be better if it were hung a while, but there's no knowing. After that it began to rain; we proceeded a little less noisily, and at last passed the bluff with which we had been playing hide-and-seek. The thought of our warm blankets securely travelling in the waterproof sheets consoled us as we sat shiver-

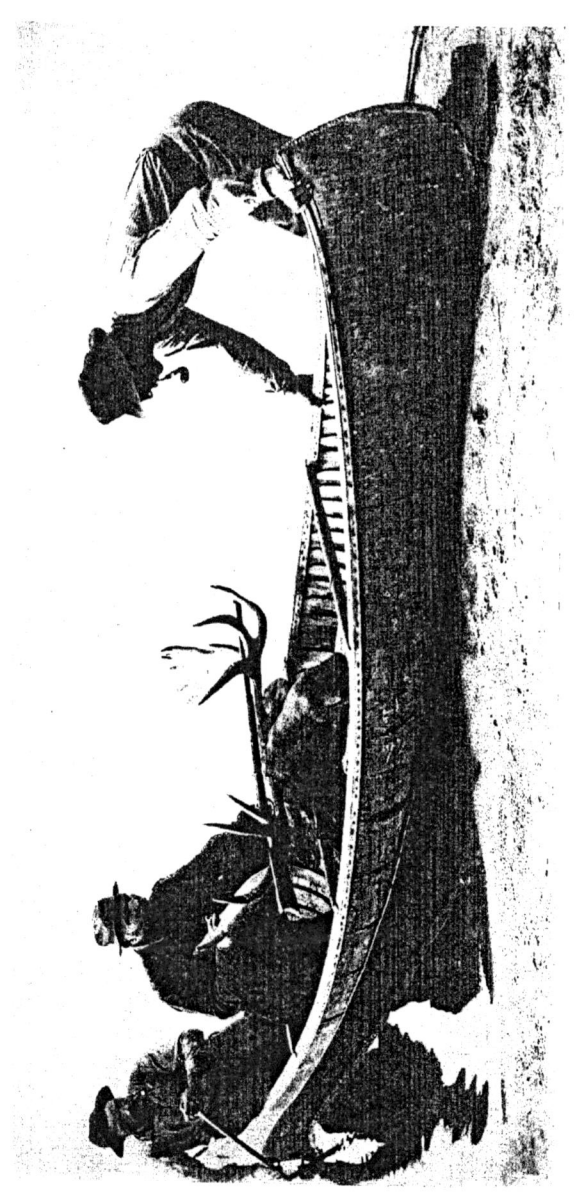

ing in the wet, thinking how presently we would be
snug and warm and laughing again. Suddenly the
bow Indian turned round with a cross click in his
throat; we looked ahead—another log jamb. The
sight sapped our energies, we could never portage
all round that in the rain, so said we would just
camp there. We drew into the gravel bank, and as
we grew near I saw a decrepit canoe close to the
débris, turned upside down. I pointed it out; the
Doctor and Joe went to look at it, and then Joe said
he knew it; it belonged to the trapper who went'
away two years ago. We were all very interested,
and wondered if we could find the man; he would
be full of information about the country by this time.

" Presently we saw a trail in the bush, and with
one accord we followed it for about a hundred yards
into the wilderness; there we saw a little clearing,
and in the middle a log hut."

I sit up, the Young 'un has stopped fidgeting, I
feet at last we are near drama, and applaud to
myself the strange method of delivery, so reserved,
so aware. The white eye-lashes do not lift, the
voice drones along—

" By the edge of the clearing was a pit, where he
had dug the clay to caulk the seams of his hut and
make it watertight. We advanced soberly; he did

not expect callers, and might be morose. The lonely life of a trapper develops strange characteristics. The door was open and the little room looked empty, but we knocked civilly. There was no answer, and the Doctor stepped in, followed by Joe Eskimo —they had to step down into the shack, and they reported no one there. The place was so dark we had to send Joe for a candle. Evidently the trapper had moved farther on. We peered about; there was his bed in one corner, I stumbled over a pair of snow-shoes, and then Joe came in with a candle, showing how low the roof was and how bare the place; there was no food anywhere, but there was an old gun in one corner. As we grew used to the dancing candlelight we saw that a tam-o'-shanter peered over the blankets on the bed. . . . The Doctor pulled back the clothes and said, ' Here, Joe, we'd better bury this.'

" There is nothing there but a skeleton. Something finished him—starvation or scurvy. We took blankets and all; there were eight pairs, so he must have died in cold weather. When we lifted him, tam-o'-shanter and skull fell back. We buried him in the pit he dug himself."

With true dramatic instinct he makes to go at this point, but I am curious and interested, and try to keep him, questioning. He will not stay, he goes to the smoking-room to join the Doctor, and the Young 'un tells me the rest of the story.

"Presently Joe came back to the river looking very business-like—he had brought the gun, and treated it gingerly, so we guessed it was loaded. It was a breech-loader, an old, old Enfield. He tied it to a tree and fixed on to it a long piece of rope, then he went as far as he could and let it off. It did not burst, and we laughed at his elaborate precautions. It made him very cross. By and by we were all at the river-side again in the pouring rain— the Doctor had the old trapper's snow-shoes with him—they were of martin-hide, and the right heel-place was neatly darned with string so white that they were evidently never worn after. I guess we didn't want to camp there with that poor devil only just getting a taste of mother earth, so we had to portage round that jamb after all. Presently it stopped raining, and we tramped on less miserably. We tramped and paddled several miles before, exhausted, we camped at last. And then we could not sleep. We lay thinking—thinking—of how the moon would shine on a new grave—of how this hot gush of pity was all too late to help him—and then through the night came a fearful sound—our flesh

crept, our blood ran cold—a noise like hounds bay-
ing to the moon, only something shriller—here was
the trapper's dirge, the howling of wolves made a
fitter keening than any of our civilized imaginings
could have given him."

We talk over the unlucky trapper, and I look at
the snow-shoes, musing on his lonely life, wondering
how he died, what had been his last thoughts alone
in that untrodden wild; what strange beasts had
borne him strange companionship in his long sleep.
I ask if they found the Falls.

"Oh yes! we found them five days later. They
are about fifty miles up Steel River from Mountain
Lake. They are about a hundred feet wide and
thirty-five feet high, in a gorge with thick bush all
round; the river falls beautifully over granite. We
named them Trapper's Falls, and I hope they'll be
called that when they come to be put on maps. After
all, why shouldn't we name them? We found them.
It took us a very short time to come back, the currents are so strong, and the Indians managed the
canoes so beautifully. And if any one doesn't believe this let him go the same trip. When he reaches
the log jamb beyond the granite bluff he'll see the
trail the trapper cut into the wilderness."

He gives me their address in Chicago and says he

will send photographs. They get off the train in the night, and I can ask no more questions. I betake myself to the end of the car and watch the landscape, happy in its moving beauty, though no more genial fellow-travellers come to tell me dramatic tales in cold, level voices that stop at the most exciting moment and refuse to talk any more.

CHAPTER V

ONTARIO, with its rocks and rivers, lakes and ravines, merges into the flats of Manitoba, and I find myself one evening, after days and nights of travelling, standing on the rear platform of the train looking at pasture-land and wheat-land, at rich farms on black soil, and I know that my eyes at last are looking on the prairie lands, the wheat-lands of the world.

Beside the interest of the farms and the lives of the farmers' wives, which I am to learn on the prairies, I feel that Winnipeg is nothing. Yet her spell falls on me before I leave; great rich metropolis of the West, where one tastes for the first time the unforgettable sweetness of Western hospitality.

An old Englishman and an old successful settler, one Mr. Larcombe, comes to fetch me from Winnipeg to spend a week on his farm, which is eight hours by train away from the city. For hours and hours after we leave Winnipeg the train jogs through a golden desert, gold skies hot and hard, golden stubble pitilessly reflecting the glare, gold stooks of wheat piled in golden perspective—unbroken plains of gold.

I look out at the little wooden house, at the shallow creeks and occasional bluffs of maple that have been planted for wind-breaks. When we come to grass instead of grain, the eye revels in its motion, grateful for a change from the yellow stubble. I had imagined the prairie dull and lifeless, but this short-flowing grass, that wimples in the wind like a coolie's coat, is full of motion and grace. There is no monotony in it, any more than there is monotony in the flowing of a river. We pass the greatly advertised Portage Plains, where they first found wheat would grow on the prairie. Twenty years ago this was the first place to build a grist mill; in these days farmers would come on a five days' journey from home to get their wheat ground, and would take the flour back, baking their bannocks by the way, and hoisting their carts out of the sloughs in the road as a matter of course, a ten days' journey in all! Those historic acres are fat and smiling enough now, and the roads are firm. A man at the other end of the car is reading aloud to his wife in a sing-song voice; nobody notices him.

On and on through the golden plains till at last the landscape breaks into bluff and scrub, it swells gently and dips here and there—the change is very grateful to the vision aching at the interminable flats. The train draws up at Birtle, and I am driven away to my host's farm in a "rig." He was a Devonshire man originally, and instinct or old association has made him settle on a beautiful wooded and undulating part of the prairie. We drive with a wild wind clean on the face, away in the whispering bush blue jays are calling. After welcome, and tea, I go out on to the farm. Sunset fading has given place to moonlight; from the corral a gentle swish-swish of milk foaming into the pails; by the side of the trail the wolf-willow shines ghostly grey. Interested and weary I wander from byre to house watching my host's daughters take the milk to the separator, watching their healthy faces, wondering why the prairies are empty of women. The pastoral life, clean and fresh and sweet, has its appeals to some women surely.

When I come down to breakfast at eight the next morning I realize with shame that I am the last, every one else has been up some hours; outside "Billy" is hitched to the rig—I am to be "driven round," it appears, and Billy turns upon me a festive eye. He knows better than I do what a drive round means. He is the most embroidered three-year-old

I have ever seen; his chest and quarters have learned too nearly the manners of wire-netting fences.

We take the trail and drive on for fifteen miles or so between green belts of bush, between aisles of Michaelmas daisies, with gophers and brilliant snakes scudding out of our path, and the wild hawk hovering overhead. We pass numberless acres of wheat, but thirty to thirty-five per cent. of the land in this district is lying dormant, and I ask why. It appears that the greater number of land-seekers who come to the West take the main line trains to Brandon, Regina, Calgary, Edmonton and through to the Coast, ignoring or never hearing of this district, to the great disgust of the loyal Birtleites, who say that they have an excellent train daily each way to Winnipeg, which is a big consuming centre. It seems such a just grievance that I hasten to ventilate it, and hope the empty acres near Birtle will be quickly peopled in consequence. It would be a splendid place for poultry farming; half-a-million dollars went to Ontario last Christmas for poultry; and it is an ideal situation and soil for market gardening. This by the way. We are seeking "Willie's farm." All the trails seem alike, and they have a fatal regularity; I sit stiffly erect in the tiny seat, which looks to my European eyes so totally out of proportion to the big spidery wheels. I rejoice in the vast distances, in the intimate way that human life presses here on to the very breast of Nature. I wonder why more Englishwomen do not come out instead of leading the crowded, hopeless lives they do in the old country. "Billy" flicks his long tail joyously over his tattered hide in answer to my thoughts. "They won't come," he seems to say; "they will not get up and milk the cows while the dew is on the golden-rod; they will not bake bread for their men, or cook the moose-steak and wild duck and prairie chicken. Your women will not come, for they love the life of cities, the typewriters, the ledgers, the proof-sheets, the palette and the stage. They do not want this life!" Billy's contemptuous flick is assuming in my eyes the proportions of a harsh judge who unfortunately has right on his side. I glance furtively at the man beside me. He is a burly Manitoban farmer, who began life in England as a farm-lad at ninepence a week. Ninepence! Now he is rich in house and land and cattle, in pigs and horses and poultry and money. But he has never hankered for cities, or got up at eight, or shirked an hour's work, I am sure. All England seems smitten and scorned as this man's life talks to me in every line of his shrewd, strong, weather-beaten face—from his

hard strong hands, in his air of self-trust. Toil speaks, toil ungrudged and unremitting, but splendidly rewarded. I feel that he is the exception, not the rule, among my countrymen; and there burns in me a kind of national shame—the same hateful thing that scorches one in the Canadian cities where obtains the legend on business houses, " No Englishmen need apply."

Here is " Willie's farm." They have begun threshing; out on the golden plain stands a monster of iron and steel with two funnels; from one funnel blows straw, from the other pours grain into a large granary. The engines whizz and whirl, an endless procession of wains piled with golden stooks pass before the monster, delivering into its jaws each its golden burden, and as they empty they pass to the fields to gather more. (A " field " may be a mile long, but that is beside the point.) The heap of straw away on the stubble is piling higher with every moment; the smaller pile of grain is growing, every inch higher means money, money means more land, more grain, *more* money. I watch the grain stream rattling out of the funnel with fascinated eyes. Every two or three seconds there is a clatter up above where the automatic weigher releases 30 lbs., then the brown stream of grain rushes down to join the rest. "Willie" also watches for a minute or so, but he shows no excitement; he is used to hearing the world's bread rattle in his granaries; his only interest seems at the moment to be focussed on the grade of his crops, he hopes for a " No. 1, Northern," and my companion in the rig, who has been critically examining a handful, votes it to be a "good No. 2." A fair-haired, blue-eyed giant comes up holding out a horny hand : "You'm from t'ould country, miss, they tell me; how's she get'n' on?"

"She's very well, thank you," I answer. "How do you like Canada?"

He smiles. "None too bad, none too bad." Later I learn that he is a "worker" and is sure to get on; any man or woman who will work here can make money.

And here and now I would like to say this, that the unsuccessful immigrant in Canada is the man who will not work. Those who will stay on the land, *and work*, cannot help getting on. I do not care who tells me in the future that he has failed out here, I shall know him for a shirker. There are millions of acres yet to be tilled, thousands of farmers who will pay well for work, who are crying for labour. I can well conceive that to the spoiled child of teeming cities, the "skilled worker," accustomed to music-halls and gin-palaces, these wide, unbroken plains of waving wheat are eminently distasteful. The artisan, accustomed to his beer and his grievance, inured from youth to the daily impact of thousands of lives upon his own life, may well feel lonely in the bush or on the prairie, but if he is not prepared to adjust himself to his new conditions and work honestly for the reward which is bound to come, he is better away. Canada has no use for him. If he cannot still his craving for the noise and light and artificial life of cities, let him stay in England where our older civilization permits of these luxuries.

We get into the rig again, but not till I have searched out the giant and fervently wished him luck, aye, and pressed his rough hand with a warmer heart than he would guess, for he is an Englishman who will not make the name of his country to stink in the nostrils of the land of his adoption. Off we go under the wide blue skies through miles of wheat, miles of scrub and bush, miles of virgin prairie damascened with purple daisies and golden-rod to Foxwarren, an ambitious little township, very prosperous and proud of itself, where I learn the secrets of a wheat elevator. I see the wagon-load of threshed grain driven on to the "dump," I see the wagon tip backwards, pouring its load into the " pit," from whence it is " elevated " in little buckets on the dredge system, into the cleaner, where poor grain, alien seeds and all dust are blown away. Thence it passes, purified for market, into a hopper and is weighed. Finally it is elevated again and dumped into "bends," or railway cars, for transportation. The "bend" is a receptacle in which a farmer may store his wheat from the close of navigation till the spring, unless he prefers to sell it outright to the Elevator Company. The waste from the cleaning process averages from one to one and a half per cent., and the farmers take it all back for hog and chicken food. It proves an interesting visit; I had seen the ugly elevators constantly on the prairies, and thought them an eyesore to be regretted. After this they mean to me thousands of bushels of grain, the harvest of the year, the farmer's glory.

We go into a homestead for tea. The farmer's wife is a busy, rather silent woman with four children; her face is nice to look at with its harsh mouth and gentle eyes. That mouth looks as though it had tasted trouble and found it bitter; her eyes, a little tired, but so kind, look as though she has much love in her life. " It's rather a busy time just at harvest,"

she says; "you must please excuse if you find things rough."

"I should think you are always busy," I reply.

"Yes," she says, "when it's not cooking it's washing; when washing's done there's ironing, and what with the housework and children and sewing and dairy and all, I have no time to spare."

"Do you do all that without help?" I ask, marvelling.

"Yes," she says, "there's no help to be got out West; I could keep a girl, too, if there was one to be had. She would soon pay for herself out of the extra butter I would be able to make. I have to keep the cows down small now, but I like a big herd. I had a girl once from the old country, but she married in a month. They always get married." She sighs, and I am silent. I know she has touched on one of the great problems of the West—the dearth of female labour.

Back to Mr. Larcombe's farm—across twenty-five miles of prairie, purple and gold, with the warm, wild wind on our faces and the wild hawk overhead. From there I wander over many hundreds of miles of prairie, by rail and rig, through many weeks, watching, noting, questioning the conditions of life which British women are so loath to accept, apparently, since they are so scarce. I sketch people and places as I find them, generally at the time and on the spot. Before I go on with the prairie studies I think I will quote an article, "to be continued," which appeared in a certain *T. P.'s Weekly*, by "A Transplanted Englishwoman." Here it is—

"Frances" spoke truly in a recent article when she said that no girl should go to the Colonies without having some idea of the conditions of life she will find there. I would, however, suggest that a cheaper and more practical method of gaining experience than by taking a course at Swanley College could be had by spending three months as a working member of the household of an English or Scotch agricultural labourer. Provided choice is made of a cottage many miles away from towns and villages, where the wife has to make her own bread and see to a few animals, I think most of the conditions of colonial life (I speak of Canada) can be experienced. These conditions can be roughly summed up as discomfort, inconvenience, and "doing without." Every labourer's wife is well inured to these conditions, and for this reason I would never have the slightest hesitation in advising a working-class woman to go to the Colonies, whereas I cannot think of one middle-class woman of my acquaintance at home whom I would care to bring out here—that is, to live as wife, sister, or daughter on a homestead.

People at home talk vaguely of "roughing it in Canada." That sounds somewhat romantic, and calls up visions of cowgirls flying across the prairie on horseback, picturesque in wide-brimmed hats and loosely-knotted neck-scarfs —red for choice. I will endeavour to put into cold, unromantic words what "roughing it" really means for the middle-class woman. Let us first take the house prepared for her by her male relative. It is of logs, and looks somewhat picturesque in a painting. As a matter of fact, dirt appears to her—especially if she arrives in spring—to be its most prominent feature. Mud is ankle deep, and the cow and chickens are wandering around the back door, adding to the filth there accumulated.

In time, of course, there will be added a fence, but at present the male relative has so many things to do. The spaces between the logs are chinked with moss, and then plastered with a clay-and-sand cement which at intervals cracks and drops off in bits, having to be done each autumn. Inside the bare logs have been covered with building-paper—the colour of a grocer's sugar-bag, yellowish-white—tacked on in somewhat unsightly fashion. Flies and spiders find a cosy home in the moss behind the paper, and frequently there are worse things. The roofing of the house is of boards and tar-paper, and by the second summer it begins to leak, so that whenever it rains it is necessary to put pots and pans under the drips. The most unpleasant places for these drips are the stove and the beds. On the prairie, where the houses are frequently roofed with sods, the drips consist of liquid mud. Of course, in the fulness of time the male relative will get the house shingled, but—he has so many things to do.

The floor, of course, is bare, the boards are unplaned and uneven, and there are large gaps between them in places. The native Canadian drudge laboriously scrubs her floor, but no sane woman who can scrape up a dollar wherewith to buy floor-paint need do this. A painted floor is easily cleaned with mop or wash-cloth. The house generally consists, for the first few years, of one large room, a part of it partitioned or curtained off for a bedroom. An Englishman will generally stand out for a board partition, for it is unpleasant to be having a bath or lying ill in bed with nothing but a curtain between one and the living-room, which is practically open to any passer-by who calls at the door. There is a door on each side of the living-room —no passage or porch between door and outside world—so that every one who goes in or out, when the temperature ranges from zero to forty-five below zero, gives those inside a taste of the fine bracing air out of doors. Those who suffer from cold feet, in spite of felt boots and three pairs of stockings, do well to comfort themselves with the thought that in six or seven months the warm weather will have come, and it will be pleasant to have open doors. At the approach of winter one cuts old coats and trousers into strips, and laboriously tacks them down the cracks in the boards of which the doors are composed, for, having been made in a hurry out of green wood, they have, of course, warped and begun to gape.

In many cases one of the worst discomforts on a new homestead is the incessant trouble about water. This is one of the numerous points we have in common with the old country agricultural labourer's wife. Time was when I thought —with my class—that "poor people" could at least keep themselves and their houses clean, for water was cheap. I know better now. In some parts of the West the water is so alkaline as to be unfit for either washing or drinking, and even the well-to-do farmers have to be dependent on rain-water in a cistern. In the bush, however, water is good and plentiful if means are taken to secure it, but the homesteader, as a rule, digs a shallow well at first, instead of going to the trouble and expense of boring. In a dry season it probably runs dry, and one goes to a neighbour's for drinking-water, and waits for rain to provide washing-water. This is in summer. From November to April one melts snow to provide all the water required for drinking, for washing, and for such animals as are kept. This is a tedious and messy process, for a pail of snow will only make half a pailful of water.

It will be understood that a bath under such conditions becomes a luxury, and one is never so wasteful as to throw away the water after one's weekly tub. It serves to mop or wash the floors on cleaning day, or to soak the dirtiest of the clothes on washing day. In time, of course, the male relative will provide an adequate water supply, but—he has so *many* things to do, and, besides, he hopes to build a proper house in a few years' time, and when he bores he will prefer to do it near the new house. Washing day in winter comes round all too quickly. It is prefaced by melting numerous pailfuls of snow, until one gets half a barrelful of water. There are, of course, no coppers in Canadian houses, either in the cities or in the new countries, and the water is heated in a tin boiler on the stove. If one is short of pails and tubs, one must just carry dirty water out in the midst of operations from a steamy atmosphere to the arctic temperature outside, and before the clothes can be shaken out to hang on the line they freeze stiff. One, of course, learns to manage things so as not to go outside until everything is finished, shaken out, and put in position to hang out as expeditiously as possible, and one puts on coat and warm gloves before starting the hanging-out performance.

Such discomforts as being many miles from a

village and post office, of doing without various articles of food, such as fresh meat in summer, milk if one has no cow, and fresh vegetables for eight months in the year one soon gets accustomed to, just as one gets accustomed to eating in the same room as one cooks in, finding everything in the house frozen solid on January and February mornings, and keeping muslin and wire mosquito- and fly-screens over doors and windows in summer. It is, of course, quite unnecessary to lengthen out on the things which every woman *must* be able to do in rural Canada, and this applies to the civilized old settled districts as well as to the new places. She must cook, clean, wash, bake bread, make butter, milk, mend her menfolk's clothes and make her own, attend to a garden, and in summer go out every day and pick wild fruit—blueberries, strawberries and raspberries —to preserve for the winter. No tame fruit is to be had, and an average provision of preserved fruit for two people for nine months will be two hundred quarts. This is not jam, but stewed fruit put in jars which seal hermetically, and which are to be bought at every village shop in Canada.

I have many quarrels with that article. The writer advises any working-class woman to go to the Colonies—and not the middle-class women. I strongly oppose such advice. The working-class woman does not bring the intelligence to bear on domestic emergencies which a cultured woman can, out of her ignorance how can she reduce disorder to comeliness, and make the prairie home a beautiful thing? It can be done. I have seen it. Then the next generation deserves some attention. If ignorant women of our lower orders go out and marry—as they will—farmers, who are often men of decent breeding, their children will go down, not up, in the scale of progress; a woman of refinement and culture, of endurance, of healthy reasoning courage, is infinitely better equipped for the work of home-making and race-making than the ignorant, often lazy, often slovenly lower-class woman. I know; I've washed too many of them in hospital days.

Then the squalid picture of the hovel drawn by the transplanted Englishwoman galls my kibe. There *are* such shacks; no man ought to ask a woman to share one; no woman ought to be silly enough to do it, unless she chooses to deliberately, and then she ought not to grumble. There are plenty of comfortable farmhouses on the prairie

where the farmer's wife will welcome her and pay
well for help. Let the transplanted Englishwoman
go to her. She will work less hard than in the
piteous hovel described so graphically, and under
infinitely more comfortable and healthy conditions
Let her earn good money and leave that "busy male
relative" to miss her enough to build a decent house,
and board his floors, and look after the well-boring
and all the rest. Even if the male relative is her
husband I'd say the same. In fact, I would say it
more urgently—such a hovel is not fit for child-
bearing, both mother and baby would suffer. Every
woman who works, and domesticity *is* work, has a
right to ask for decent working conditions, and if
she cannot get them, to leave any man, husband or
no, and work for herself until he can provide them.
The labourer is worthy of her hire. I have no
patience with the women who go to ill conditions
and grumble about them instead of bettering them.
There is no *need* to stop and be miserable. No one
can compel you to.

I asked one woman on the prairie who slaved to
keep her shack in nice living conditions, "Aren't
you sorry you came?" She went to the door and
looked across the sunny acres. "No!" she said,
"this is all our own. England could never have
given us this. We shall soon be more comfortable."

The "transplanted Englishwoman" talks of doing without fresh vegetables for eight months in the year. There is no need for it. I have something to say on market gardening later on—but what on earth is to prevent her growing her own vegetables? The relative afore-mentioned will spare her an acre or two near the shack where she can grow "roots," as they call them over there, and store them for winter use as her neighbours do, in a cellar or "root-house."

It is bitter to find individual incompetence described as general conditions. To do the lady justice she does say in her next and concluding article that there is hope for those who stick to their drudgery—the hope of ultimate betterment.

T. P.'s Weekly, however, does not publish only grumbles. Here is a letter from a worker of evidently cheery soul who makes comfort out of what may readily be turned to hideous discomfort. A very different story this man tells.

To the Editor of " T. P.'s Weekly "

SIR,

   After living in Canada for six years, and having resided in the provinces of Ontario and Manitoba—I am now in Saskatchewan upon a farm of my own—I think I may claim to have a good knowledge of the country. Like "Successful Man," I emigrated to Canada independently, which seems to be the only way to avoid trouble. The Canadian Immigration Department specially advise against dealing with private agents and advertisements such as ended so disastrously for the "Three Who Failed."

Arriving at Winnipeg, I applied at the Government Bureau for a position, and was sent out to a country town in Manitoba with a letter of introduction to the postmaster, asking him to place me with some farmer needing help. Unfortunately, this old postmaster got in a temper, saying he had "no connection with the Immigration Department." However, he stated the case to some farmers that had just called for their mail. They told me of a man whom they thought needed help. As I had only thirty cents in my pocket and was practically stranded, and night drawing near, I of necessity paid the farmer a visit. His hospitality was all that could be desired, and, after keeping me overnight—I suppose to "size me up," for I was pale-faced and anything but sturdy-looking—told me he did not really need a man, but directed me to another farmer; and, after walking fifteen miles from place to place, I finally obtained a position at fifteen dollars per month.

I was not altogether "green" at farm work, but being new to the country was to my disadvantage, and Canadian farmers, like most employers, will not pay any more than they can help. After serving six months in my first berth I changed from place to place, always getting highest wages—fifteen dollars for winter and thirty dollars for summer. I always selected the larger farms, for on them they usually have some system and pay highest wages, and a man learns quicker. On the small farms, where there is only one man, he has everything to do; system is lacking, which often makes the working hours long. I have worked on large farms of 2,000 acres and upwards with as many as ten other men, each having four horses under his care and to work.

"Successful Man" said he "always avoided the bachelors" because of their "wretched establishments and the absence of female help." It is true some of them are negligent, but not all of them are as black as he has painted them. I myself am a bachelor, not through choice, but rather force of circumstances, and know the situation only too well. I am constrained to put aside my natural modesty to modify the statement that in "these establishments" there are "no properly-cooked meals, no regular hours, general disorder, dirt, etc." I have known many to be systematic, orderly, and excellent cooks; and some I have known to receive great praise at the hands of women for their household management. Recently I had a threshing machine with a crew of sixteen men (and this is the average number in the West) to do my threshing; and I had to do all the cooking alone for them for three meals. Through force of circumstances I have become fairly proficient in this art, though this is the first time I have been put to so severe a test.

As to the absence of women, which "Successful Man" mentions, it is not the fault of the bachelors. The bachelors are a great majority, and the women are not in the country. Any woman who ventures here will receive more than her share of attention, and, most likely, be promptly appropriated by some bachelor anxious for a happier state. The crying need

of Western Canada is women; it is like that heathen cry which comes to the missionary— "Come over and help us." Though Canada is not altogether "heathen," it needs the missionary spirit of women to make it a crowning success, and no doubt many of the teeming multitude of British women would profit by this golden opportunity. The life, though strenuous, is not altogether monotonous, for one can have one's hours of leisure in which to cultivate the mind as well as the land, if the man so desires.

Yours faithfully,

J. G. S., Sask., Canada.

That man deserves a good wife! I have lingered to quote and comment because there is so much written one way and another on the prairie farm-life that English readers must often be rarely puzzled to know what to believe. Every one writes sincerely, I think, from the individual point of view. Every reader may be sure that in himself alone is the stuff to make this picture of Canada come true, or that.

CHAPTER VI

.THE trail is what one might call hummocky, the heat is fierce, and I am getting my skirt covered with grease from a new kind of cartridge. My face and hands I gave over to perdition after the first ten minutes with them, but the extension of damage to my skirt is less easy to bear as I am "travelling light," and it will be ten days before I reach Calgary and my trunk!

The little smokeless bullets I used at first were hardly big enough to kill, and after I had suffered seeing half-a-dozen little furry gophers die slowly in great rebellion, I open a box of black-powder cartridges and become a pillar of grease!—and mercy. I am really driving out over this sun-smitten prairie to see an Englishwoman who has newly settled in Canada, and learn from her of the conditions, but the journey is considerably gilded by the loan of a ·22 Winchester and the presence of a driver who connives at gopher-shooting. We dawdle along and shoot from the rig whenever the boy turns with a " Say ! there's a dandy shot," and I see a pretty squirrelly person sitting by his hole staring defiance with his cheeks bulged with stolen wheat. I would recommend gophers to any one who prefers a rifle to a shot-gun—they give quite as good sport as rooks in May, and that is saying a good deal. We lose our way once and I am electrified to find a patch of prairie roses in bloom. They are the loveliest things of wonder, in that desert of scorched grass—from dead white to deep red they grow on low bushes a foot or so high and smell with a wild, warm sweetness impossible to describe; we find the trail again and see at last the place we are looking for. Out on the livid grass it stands, a mean black shack of wood and pulp-paper, a lowlier shelter than many a farmer's beast would have in England. My heart sinks with pity as we approach—how can anybody live in such a shell here in this arid, treeless desert? The rig draws up and a man comes out of the doorway, I get a glimpse into a stifling den of flies, and am reminded of the accommodation in a gipsy's caravan—this looks no bigger. There is a small tent in front of the shack—I suppose for sleeping in in dry weather. The man listens to my story and takes me round to

see his wife; he is a nice man, deeply tanned, with
humorous eyes and a strong chin. I like his face.
His wife is sitting the other side of the shack in the
shade, nursing a fat baby. As I sit beside her I am
wholly prepared for an outburst of grumbling, and,
indeed, I feel I have no right to expect anything
else. But lo! like the roses in the gasping prairie
there blooms nothing but courage and cheerfulness
from her tale.

"Lonely! not a bit now I have my baby! But
even without him there was plenty to do. A farmer's
wife in Canada must expect work. In seeding-time
she will be up at 4 a.m. to get the men their breakfast. Then she will have to milk, and separate the
cream afterwards, if they have a separator. If there
are several cows it is quite a back-aching task.
Then there will be the house to clean, the breakfast
things to wash up, the beds to make, and she must
not waste time over that part of her day for there is
dinner to cook for hungry men by 11.30. After
washing up again the afternoon will mean bread-
making, or clothes-washing and ironing, or jam-
making, or butter-churning—one of the endless
things like that anyway, and at 7.30 or 6.30 (accord-
ing to the season of the year) she must have "tea"
ready. Tea is nearly as big a meal as dinner and

the last meal of the day. After that she must wash up, then milk two cows and separate her cream before she can think of going to bed. Probably there will be some darning or mending to do even then. That is a straightforward day, but it is greatly complicated when the children begin to come."

She has told me the tale of labour quite simply. Her eyes are happy, her face is beautiful with health and courage.

"We only came out a year ago," she continues; "in a week or two we will move into a good house— this is very uncomfortable—my husband has bought another farm and it has a house on it. Isn't my boy beautiful? but he was born before his time. You wouldn't think so, would you? I had to go so far to reach the hospital that the journey upset me, and I was very afraid for him, he was nearly a month too soon."

The baby is a magnificent chap, worthy of unstinted praise and gets it, though he dislikes my way of holding him and clamours to get back to the arms he is growing to know. "Do you think he will smile at me soon?" she says. "I am so glad to have him, but the women suffer much out here in these wilds for lack of proper nurses. They want qualified midwives who will turn to when their patients are settled, and do housework for them. It is a dreadful thing to know how many prairie women go through their confinements alone; I was very lucky, I was able to get to a hospital, but lots of them can't." I ask her if she is homesick for the old country, and she saddens for a second. "Will one ever lose that feeling, I wonder? It will come all right. We are getting on, we are not going to give in—we have never thought of doing that."

The man comes out of the shack with tea and bread and butter for me—he has prepared it all quietly while I was talking; as he returns to his work the young wife watches him very fondly. "Englishmen make better husbands than Canadians," she announces, and I observe that the latter would not like to hear her say so. We laugh and talk on about the life, the people, the country.

I discern in her a reserve of cheerfulness that promises success for both in the venture. Her laughter is not forced, it bubbles continually from some inner fount of joy. They came from the Midlands, and neither of them understood land culture, in general a foolhardy experiment. But these two young English people are on a fair way to success—I cannot exactly say why. They may be intelligent above the average, they may have brought considerable capital, they may, or he may, own to some streak of farmer blood which helps him to learn readily, it may be unusual industry (a quality which always brings success in Canada), or it may be—who knows?—that old-fashioned love has them in grip, and makes everything seem easy for each other and nothing too hard to win. I have pictured them exactly as I found them—I cannot hit on what made them so interesting and so nice in their squalid shack. I only know that their eyes were kind when they looked at each other, and they were very happy in surroundings which many would have bitterly resented. I realize one thing as I look at them and say "Good-bye"—the hardness of a settler's lot is infinitely lessened if he has a wife to smile with him. A grumbling woman could have made life hell for both on that blazing, shadeless plain.

If I were to come next year I should see them in a nice house, with granaries and cow-sheds; with more acres of prairie broken into grain, and a small fat person toddling round who has learned to smile at mother.

Going, I sniff industriously—it almost feels as if I can smell mignonette! I accuse them inwardly

of having made me homesick with their peaceful
English voices; but a few yards from the shack *I*
see a plaintive tribute to our common nationality—
a square yard, not more, of prairie land hedged
round with pegs and string, where bloom gloriously
mignonette and nasturtium.

    *   *   *   *   *   *

    I am prepared to write Canada down a tropical
country! This is mid-September and the heat is
fierce; the train ambles along over a new wobbly
track—the passengers have long ago given up resist-
ance and are lying or sitting, gasping, in every
position of wretchedness. Some of us are sitting
on the end of the car, blinded with dust and glare,
but getting some slight draught from the motion of
the train. I am on my way to an old settler's farm
—they came out sixteen years ago, have done well,
and belong to the type of moneyed farmers now.
The train brings me at last to the station of a little
prairie township, and there a burly man with a red
face claims me with a hospitable grunt.

    " It's very good of you to meet me," I say politely.
"You must be busy at this time of year? "

    "Yes," he says, "we'm busy. Mind that step.
It's deceitful. More slips off than gets on with it."

    I make for the step gingerly. It is a very little

one behind a big wheel, and I "slip off it as most do," to the great discomfort of my shins. When I get fixed, the horses turn towards the sunset and we drive in a fairy world of amethyst light, creek and bush and slough mantled in purple and gold. The farmer is pleased with my admiration.

"You should see this 'ere in spring," he says, "when acres of purple crokers bloom wild over the prairie, and them tiger-lilies and wild roses and that maiden'air fern they think such a lot of in the ould country; sakes! you'd oughter see it then."

He tells me of the early struggles. He was a cobbler in England and went into farming where he was "beggared by a little farm of nine acres at a rental of £3 an acre." Now he has 1,500 acres of *his own land* and "money in the bank," besides stock. But the early struggles were hard; they would have gone back to England scores of times if they had had the money, he says. At first he worked hard only to make money to pay the passage back; but hard work brought the reward of this country, money—more money than he had ever handled before, and he determined to stay on and see if he could not go back with a few thousand dollars. Now he tells me he could not live anywhere in the world but this free North-West.

The farmhouse proves to be a large building of brick—a sign in itself of prosperity, at the door a short, stout lady in gorgeous apparel beams affably. "The missus," he says shortly, "and the lady from England." The missus and the lady shake hands, and I see her eyes travel in acute disappointment over my plain linen dress and Panama hat. I follow her into the house humbly conscious that I have fallen short of a preconceived ideal of what the "lady from England" should look like. We go into the parlour, a realm of fumed oak chairs and violent cretonnes, garrulous with pink and blue flower-vases and "knick-knacks," and there we sit stiffly, discussing the weather and politics. I learn that "my 'usbind is a Conservative and don't 'old with them grafters at all." Also that "Mrs. Warren and Mrs. Suter called on me this afternoon, or I would a' come to meet you." This with some pride. I wonder vaguely if a "grafter" is a Socialist or a Liberal, and how my hostess has time for calling or being called upon in this busy land. The room is very stuffy and does not seem to have been dusted for some time. Grievous odours of cooking assail the air; I long to be allowed to go out on the "lawn" (a patch of prairie grass) and look at the petunias, which riot in confusion everywhere. But

124

conversation drags on, every now and then a daughter of the house will come in and sit for a moment, looking at me with her hands folded on her lap. Then she returns to the region of smells. (I want to see the ordinary daily life and this is not at all what I came for.) By and by we go in to "tea"—a heavy meal of ham and cold beef, honey and jam, cakes and tea. The whole family is there, including the farm-hands; every one helps himself —the flies most of all—and I suffer several shocks. Food is here in plenty, but carelessly served— dirtily served. I endure agonies of conscience as the farm-help near me takes a fly-blown slice of beef on his fork from the common dish in the centre of the table. Ought I to tell him? Or is he used to it? Would my hostess be hurt? Is it my duty to hurt her and tell her the beef is not fit to eat? While the dispute rages within the farm-help has eaten his beef, and I resign him to his fate. The tablecloth is very dirty, the butter has not been put in the ice safe (an unpardonable sin in Canada, where every household has its store of ice gathered in winter). I drink a cup of tea and plead a head-ache for lack of appetite. After the meal is over I volunteer to turn the "separator," to the great surprise of "Missus," who, I am sure, thinks I have never done an hour's work in my life. But I am again badly shocked. The separator is near the kitchen stove, a very inferno, and the last place for milk to be in this weather. ,The flies make high holiday, for the wire-netted door is propped wide open instead of being kept shut; the pails are none too clean, the strainer is certainly *not* clean. I feel I want to scald every vessel in the place, to pack ice round the milk corner, and to kill every fly, to scrub the greasy, dingy floor, and box the ears of Missus and her tribe of feckless daughters. This is an experience indeed. Here I am finding the farmer's wife as she should not be; a woman of plebeian stock who, with prosperity, is greedily clutching the worst features of the class above her, which claims all the admiration of her foolish, snobbish soul.

She must wear a silk blouse—and "call" of an afternoon forsooth—and neglect her home for society. I retire to bed wrathful and perplexed.

After an hour in bed an odious suspicion presents itself. It increases in virulence and becomes a certainty. I consider the touch of an unclean insect an affront—it is a thing I refuse to tolerate. With ludicrous precautions against the acquisition of one of the creatures I dress and creep downstairs to sleep on the "lawn." For three hideous days I live on tea and toast, sleeping on the lawn at night when every one else has gone to bed, and rising before any one is up to avoid discovery. Then I resist all invitation to prolong my visit, and take train for a farm six hundred miles away where I am going to study conditions in the house of an English settler and his wife, neither so new as the first nor so old-established as these last.

As I drive away, pursued by cordial good-byes (for the Missus has forgiven me my low-born taste for farm-work and hatred of "calling"), I muse on the pity of it all. These people are rich, they could have their house cleaned, papered, painted—they could afford to hire servants to keep it nice if such were to be found in the district and they didn't want to work themselves; they have no excuse for dirt but one—they don't know any better. They come of a poor old-country stock, bred probably for hundreds of years in poverty and dirt, ignorance and class-worship. They don't know any better. And the pity is for the land of their adoption.

*　*　*　*　*　*

I am sitting beside my "good, reliable driver" in the hired single rig, which is to take me to a farm on the Eagle Hills fifteen miles away. I have especially described the kind of driver I want as experience has taught me the grief of trusting to unskilled pilots among the sloughs and mud-holes on the prairie trails; instinct tells me that this good-looking young man, with his fiery eye and casual acceptance of my directions, is hardly up to my description. I wonder whether to make a fuss and ask at the livery stable for another, but decide against, probably he is all right. So off we go at an easy lope to follow Red Pheasant trail. The ferry is crowded with oxen and wagons, with rigs and " democrats "; true it is that the mare prefers the side of the trail to the middle of it and we ride most of the way at a fearful angle, but the sun holds us in such kind regard, and the blue harebells fling such a frail defiance to the wind that there is no room for anything but happiness. If it were possible I would describe the country, but there is no way. I am unable to show to English minds the wide Western horizon, the height and blueness of the skies, the stinging caress of the wind, sweet with scent of the upland hay and the wild charm of the prairie when it breaks, as it does here, into rolling dunes of grass and scrub. Between the little hills lie broad blue lakes—I had thought Manitoba beautiful, now I am fain to forget her in Saskatchewan. Wind and sky and lonely spaces . . .

there is that in the West which will make my heart bleed to leave it. . . . The afternoon wears on, the sun plunges behind the hills and I begin to realize that the mare is slacking wearily, the air is growing crisp with frost, that fifteen miles was never so long in the world, and that my "good, reliable" driver is looking round uneasily. "Are we lost?" I ask.

"Guess so," he answers, and so we are. After driving on and on we find a homestead and learn that we are nearing "Swift Current," miles from "Red Pheasant." The settler is pleased to see strangers, and keeps us a long time outside his shack while he tells us the way. The sun drops rapidly, the air grows sharper than a serpent's tooth, and I sit brooding on the pleasures of a night on the open prairie. I try to believe what the settlers say about the coyotes—that they are cowards and run away if you "shoo" them. I try to persuade myself that it will not be horribly cold, and that three oranges in my sachel will supply us with food and drink. Every now and then the mare gets us into a mud-hole or shies at an insecure log bridge. At last we find a French half-breed on a lean broncho; he tells us we are wrong again, and I ask him if we can find the place at all to-night. He thinks so if we don't go wrong any more, and I offer him a dollar to put us right. He leads us to Red Pheasant trail and we jog along for eight more miles, lit by the Northern lights, shivering miserably.

At last we see a light on the hill, we conciliate a big Newfoundland dog, and an English voice says kindly, "You are blue with the cold, now come in at once." Soon, from the security of warm sheets and woolly blankets I listen to the coyotes howling.

A step passes my door at dawn. I get up and go down-stairs; there she is—my pretty hostess with her young face and grey hair, lighting the kitchen fire for the day's work. I watch her for a little while. She has a contented face and works very neatly; her dress is a pretty blue cotton and over it is a linen apron, the sleeves are rolled to the elbow, her feet are thickly shod, she wears a low collar, her skirt is four inches from the ground, there is nothing to impede her movements, and yet the whole effect is very smart and workmanlike.

Presently she goes out and I follow her; we walk down to the corral in the tender light that hangs like a kiss on the brow of day; I watch her milk the six cows, help her feed the calves, and gather in the breakfast eggs; we linger a minute to admire the black baby pigs that race from bush to barn, sleek and ridiculous. We sympathize, at a distance, with poor Tim the terrier, who has lately killed a skunk and been shut up till he can be disinfected; we tread delicately like Agag through the dewy golden-rod to the kitchen garden, where we gather some squaw corn for breakfast, and I have time to admire the pitch of cultivation to which it has been brought,—onions, beets, celery, potatoes, carrots, cabbages, turnips, peas, beans, all growing luxuriously in the rich black loam.

"I love the garden," she says; "I do most of it myself. Aren't the sweet peas lovely? The Canadians use tinned vegetables far too much—it is not healthy, and they can grow them beautifully if they will take the trouble. They have several little faults, only I would hesitate to tell them so— they spoil their complexions and make themselves delicate by keeping their houses too hot. They think me mad because I have lots of fresh air in the house, and because my boys have a bath every day and four clean shirts a week." It is on the tip of my tongue to tell her I know of some English settlers who would think these things mad too, but I refrain. Her loyalty to the old country, so often derided out here, is too sweet to taint with shame for any of its people.

"We have been out nearly six years," she tells
me while she is preparing breakfast, talking in little
jerks while she runs from cellar to stove and stove
to table; "but my husband came out two and a
half years before me—that was a long, cruel wait
for us with only letters and photographs to live on;
he was in a city office at first, but he was too big and
strong to stand the sedentary stuffy life; after we
talked it over we decided to risk our £250 saved
for furnishing and try farming in Canada; he came
out homesteaded and made good—he worked as a
labourer first, learning the soil and the conditions
and saving money all the time. When he came to
till his own land and build his own house he was
able to profit by all he had learned, it saved him
hundreds of dollars." . . . "But the boss hasn't
told you what she was doing all the time," says her
husband, coming in from his chores; he is a fair-
haired giant of thirty-three or so and looks less like
any city man I have ever seen. "She went and
trained for a nurse, because she said the farm work
could never be as hard as hospital work and it
taught her to get up early. That was good, wasn't
it? When she started here, I tell you, she often
drove the hayrake with a pair of oxen, and I've
known her pitch hay till sundown—we're in better

shape now and doing good; she doesn't do that any more."

"It's a lovely life," she says, "everything smells fair and sweet—there are young, healthy, live things round you all the time."

The meal is fragrant with the steam of good coffee, the taste of clover honey and wild-strawberry jam, eggs so fresh that they are creamier than cream itself, golden bannocks and home-made bread, which is the crown of every settler's table! This homestead is very different from the last one. Breed has a great influence in the ordering of lives; with exactly the same materials to her hand one Englishwoman makes of her home a paradise and the other in her ignorance a smellsome hovel.

While the farmer and the farm-hands start breakfast she runs up-stairs for Humpty and Dumpty, who in due course appear, shiny and hungry, but when she has her own breakfast I don't to this moment recollect. We had ours, and they had theirs, and I suppose she had hers too, but it must have been quick. When the farmer goes out to plough fireguards round the stacks I engage the Humpty Dumpties in a miraculous fairy story, full of candy and pop-corn, while Mummy makes beds and rushes from room to room like a Utopian whirlwind that leaves order in its train. They are four and two years old, these babies; as they listen to the oracle with their round, brown eyes and curly hair widespread about their heads like haloes, I speculate on how they would have fared in England, and realize that this broad heritage, won by their parents from the wild, is a nobler gift from one generation to another than the unendowed gift of life which would have been all they would have got in the old country. 'Aye, and that gift, too, is often tainted at the spring. . . . The day is short because it is so full; her young face, brown-eyed, and rosy under its mass of grey hair, beams on me with the good nature of perfect health and high spirits, twinkling when I express astonishment at her energy, jerking out scraps of information at odd intervals.

"Jim says you can shoot some wild duck if you go with him to-morrow—we can lend you a gun— he'll be by the lake and you can get good sport while he is at work; we want some more meat." I profess modest incompetence.

"They're so thick you couldn't help hitting them, the temptation is to kill too many; prairie chicken are more difficult. No! I don't sell much butter, I could if I made more, but I do want help; there is none to be got in the West, you know; directly an

active, clever woman comes out she gets married. I wish I could find one to help me with dairy and chickens, and the pigs, they are all my 'perquisites,' and I could make a lot of money by them if I had more time. This afternoon I must make bread, and bannocks if you like them; those onions are ready for pickling, and I have all Jim's winter vests to make. I must get them cut out before the threshers come. They'll be here for two and a half days, twenty men—think of the feeding! I used up a whole hog last year. They don't mind if the service is rough so long as the food is good. Yes! we generally thresh from stack, the grain sometimes improves in colour by stacking and it's safer, too. A little rain will delay a great time if you thresh from stock." I listen to her as I wander from the dinirg-kitchen to the living-sitting-room; her taste is gcod—here are no lithographs, but plain green walls hung with the "Four Seasons," Millet's "Gleaners," Rossetti's "Beata Beatrix"; a bookcase where Scott jostles Omar, Don Quixote leans against Schopenhauer, and Dickens riots in beautiful red calf alongside Henry Harland and De Maupassant; a dado of green burlap, a small cottage piano—that is all, except for the vases of sweet peas, and the Dresden cups and saucers, choice but few, carefully carried from the old country six years ago. A restful room—I feel that to look in it is to know its owners have indeed "made good" in Canada.

I ask her about the birth of her babies. "Don't talk of it," she says; "I nearly died last time, and we thought poor Dumpty surely must die. He was born hours before the doctor came, and the nurse was away on another case thirty miles off. I was alone but for Jim, he sent the chore-boy for the doctor and he lost his way in a blizzard. Don't talk of it. We need nurses at reasonable distances all over the prairies—sensible, skilled women, but they are hard to get."

The same cry as that first woman gave! If the Dominion Government would secure to itself a fine race it must watch the needs of its mothers.

"After bread-baking we will take a walk and look at the standing wheat, if you like."

We set forth near milking-time, and walk past the gopher holes and badger holes and pale wolf-willow to the standing corn. It rustles in the wind and exudes the faintest hint of a warm grainy smell under the blazing sun; the slight harsh sound reminds me fantastically of bank notes rustling, it billows like a sea, wave on wave, acre on acre, mile on mile; timely bluffs make wind-breaks for the crop, and shine like green oases in the Sahara of growing gold. Here, where they found virgin prairie, she stands; the heavy ears lap against her splendid hips, and here and there they tip her breast; round her skirts the children cling, she moves in this beautiful, fruitful land like Ceres among plenty.

"Now, Humpty, if you look at the new Auntie over there you'll see she is making a 'mental picture,' and if you look at the sun you'll see he is making long shadows. The two don't agree. Long shadows say bed-time for little Humpties and little Dumpties, so Auntie's picture must melt away." Off home we all go like geese in single file. Beautiful big Mummy first, then fat Humpty, the sleepy Dumpty, and lastly "Auntie" making notes.

"No, it's not with the troubles of farming, if it was any trouble at all it was from living in a highly rented Putney house with a lot of brothers and sisters who needed more money than father could earn!" She has bathed the two rolls of fat and is putting them to bed. "It's hereditary—I was grey at twenty and my brother at eighteen! Do you hear the cow-bells?" I look out of the window, far away I see the tiny windmill arms of the binder flapping industriously; I hear a sleepy "Amen" followed by "Good-night" behind me.

Here is the sleek, slow herd; one by one the cows come lowing into the corral. There she is, pails in hand, going to meet them among the wolf-willow and golden-rod.

* * * * * *

My conscience stirs uneasily—in all my wanderings through this beautiful busy country I have not found an Englishwoman to tell me in close detail her experiences of Canadian domestic life as she found it on first landing, white-hot with eager industry—and ignorance. They would be useful reading, I know, to intending immigrants, and till I find them I feel I have hardly obeyed the official instructions to "describe Canada from a woman's point of view." A difficulty I have never foreseen confronts me, for the feckless settlers have nothing of value to tell, little but self-revealing grumbles to offer, and the workers have so much to do that they will hardly talk about it. It is quite near the end of my sojourn in the country before I find what I want: an English girl who came out two years ago to keep house for her brothers, and who tells her story vividly while she gets tea ready in the little wooden house out on the prairie. She is young and pretty, I watch her work with pleasure; she has curly red hair and a pleasant voice, her hands are red and rough, an honourable sign in this country. Far away on the horizon is a crimson ring of sunset, in the middle distance a straw-stack burns with a pale yellow flame.

"I'll tell you of my first day," she says. "I can never forget how odd it all was. I got to Regina at two in the morning, and whenever I think of the city I see it as I saw it then for the first time, silent and grey, with its unpretentious rows of wooden houses. My brothers had been 'batching' it, and welcomed me gladly; they are not farmers, they work in the city and had had many discomforts to put up with. I started right into work at once—I got up that same morning to make their breakfast; they were asleep still, and I wanted to please them from the first day they had me there. I went into the kitchen to make the fire, but could find no wood, no coal, no water; I looked about for the bundles of tidy sticks one always has in the old country, nothing to be seen. Then I remembered I must not expect comforts, and went outside to hunt. I found a shed with coal, but all the wood was big round pine logs, hopeless for kindlings. I hunted for a chopper. It cost me a long time and a cut finger to splinter enough for my purpose, and when I tried the stove—oh! I wish you'd seen how clumsy I was. I tried to light the fire from the front like we did at home, but I found it worked from the top, and after my eyes were smarting with smoke and my temper ruffled it began to draw. Then for the water: I looked everywhere, there was none to be found, no taps, no barrel, no anything! I took a pail and searched round about for a well, but at last had to call one of the boys and he took me down to the well that supplies several of us here— a good four hundred yards away.

"It was with real dismay that I realized how every drop of water I used must be drawn from the well and carried all that way. At last I got them some tea and bread and bacon, and sent them off to work with a list of wanted stores. We are too far from the shops to be really comfortable here. After they had gone I looked round. First to wash up the breakfast things. There was no sink, no sign of a sink; earnest search revealed a pail full of tea-leaves, potato-parings and refuse hidden behind a packing-case—evidently this must be my portable sink; but where to empty it? I went to the door and surveyed the blank prairie; at last I took a spade and dug a deep hole far from the shack, for the boys had evidently emptied the 'sink' out of the front or back door, or anywhere handy, during their reign, and the method did not commend itself to me. With a pail and tin basin I made shift to wash up; then made the beds, cleaned the dusty windows, scrubbed the kitchen floor, and then made for my great work. Early in proceedings I had spied in one corner of a room up-stairs a heap of dirty clothes, socks full of holes, tailless shirts and other bachelor signs, which made my female heart to bleed. The tablecloths looked as if they had been used to clean boots with—at least two months' washing stared me in the face. Half-a-mile or more away I spied a neighbour's shack—there I went to borrow a wash-tub after a hopeless search for the thing at home, and I first drew four pails of water up from the well, putting three of the pails straight on the stove to heat. The neighbour, a slatternly Irish woman, with tousled hair hanging about her face, and gifted with a dingy, sore-eyed child, lent me her tub with all the good-will in the world. With indescribable back-ache I washed the pile of clothes and linen from pure black to pale grey, the best I could compass, and then was hard put to for a clothes-line. At last I remembered a cord round a trunk up-stairs, and unknotted it with sodden fingers wondering where to fix it to—there was no pole, there are no trees here! Finally I strung it between the house and woodshed, and hung out the washing to dry. There was hardly any food in the place, I boiled some potatoes and made a 'hasty' pudding for my dinner. When the boys came in with the stores I prepared their supper and listened with seemly humility to their expressions of admiration and delight!"

Funny little woman with the red hair and red hands! What will the "boys" do when she marries? She has refused two offers already for their sakes, but she can hardly be expected to do that for ever. I look round me, and see how beautifully she keeps the house; outside she has rigged up a primitive boot-scraper to save her shining floors, a clothes-line stretches proudly between poles beyond the back door; endless homely contrivances bear witness to her ready wit and industry. The "boys" must marry too, in self-defence! But wives are scarce in Western Canada.

*   *   *   *   *   *

Here is a Dutch cattle-herd, who has charge of a fine dairy farm five miles from Regina. He is a big, handsome man who talks English with the same quaint haunting accent that I have always

associated with Nico Jungman. His is a splendid
herd of grades and thoroughbred Ayrshires—but,
then, it ought to be splendid. He "mothers" them
as a woman her children. The cattle are "in"—
they will be kept in from now (mid-October) till the
middle of May, going out sometimes for a few
hours on the very fine days. Only the young and
dry stock is allowed to range through the winter, the
milch cows need warmth and care—and don't they
get it! I follow him into the warm, sweet-smelling
byre where a fat grey cat prances frantically after
the prongs of his pitchfork, and there he passes
from one prize-winner to another, telling me how
each one has her different feed—this one is going
to beef and so is on bran, which does not make fat
and gives a good yield of milk; this one has oats
chopped and flaxmeal and middlings, she needs
building up; this one is off her feed and is therefore in disgrace, having her milk tested by Dr.
Charlton the bacteriologist to fix the trouble. We
look at the sturdy calves, nineteen of them all born
in the purple, and he strokes their backs, fluffy with
the coming winter coats. At a wary distance I
admire the great bull, and suffer with what dignity
I can his evident dislike of me. Cornelius Zoon
pats him familiarly, and says he is annoyed because
he "hasn't seen anything like you before." The

kindly Board of Trade official, who has driven me over to the farm, explains this hard saying. "He means that women hardly ever come here," that's all! The herd tells me of the crops—how they grow alfalfa for the calves, but do not grow hay; instead they cut the "prairie wool" (the native grass) and stack it, it is just as good as grown hay. His daily programme of average food in that byre reads like a fairy tale, in my ignorance I never guessed cows could eat so much. At 4 a.m. he gives them their first meal of bran or chop; at 6.20 an oatsheaf each; at 7.30 water; at 10 another oatsheaf; at noon more water; at 1 he gives them hay; at 4 p.m. chop; at 5.30 sheaf; at 6.30 water; at 7 hay again, and twice a week a little salt! All the while this big Dutchman is working towards ultimate independence. That is the glory of work in Canada. It has such rewards. He tells me of his half-section (320 acres), half of which he has homesteaded and the other half "pre-empted." Little by little he will build his fortunes, when he can "quit" working for hire and start altogether on his own land he will be on the way to prosperity. His round, rosy, child-like face glows as he talks, his blue eyes beam with hope.

*　　*　　*　　*　　*　　*

One of the most difficult things in life is to refute an accusation of vulgarity. Difficult because it is only the whole of oneself—that is to say, one's life, one's work, one's mental outlook—that can be called in witness for the defence. Here is a cutting which reached me on my return to England.

An Englishwoman by birth, but a Canadian by adoption, has written to the *Regina Leader*, criticizing Mrs. Cran's study of a prairie home, which was published on this page last week. She thinks Mrs. Cran must have met a very unusual class of people. She has visited many farm homes, and has never seen dirtily served food, nor has she met any farmers who did not introduce their wives. She also considers the farmer's daughter, who sits with her hands in her lap and says nothing, quite an exception, for, as a rule, farmers' daughters can talk, and talk well too. She says—

"Certainly I am amused at the vexation of Mrs. G. Cran, because the farmer's wife wears a silk blouse and receives callers. Why should she not? Surely the women who share with their husbands the isolation incumbent upon farm life may be permitted to indulge in neighbourly 'calls' and sociability, which to my mind seems better than a visit made in the interest (?) of journalism, and while accepting hospitality with outward cordiality, feeling 'wrathful' and vicious, and writing up one's host and hostess to expose their faults and failings. But while I am sorry the lady's 'journalistic industry' landed her with such undesirable 'plebeians,' I rejoice that the number of such is very small, and look forward to the time when those who have bravely worked through the early years in the Great West shall reap to the full extent all it has in store for them of reward, and satisfaction in looking back at work well done, and instead of pitying the land of their adoption I am proud of the pioneer men and women, those who have helped, and are still helping, to open up this country of wonderful possibilities. May their number increase."

It is hardly intelligent criticism, it is stupid to judge of a building by a brick. The lady judges by one of a series of studies, as those who read may see. She is first of all inaccurate; the farmer did introduce his wife, simply, shortly, but quite nicely. She misapprehends me when she gibes at my "vexation" in the matter of silk blouses and calls. The farmer's wife may wear silk blouses and silk hats and silk skirts, and sleep in silk sheets under a silken canopy, she may have callers by the gross every hour of every day with my entire approval—if that counts for anything—if she keeps her house clean, and can afford these luxuries. She says she has visited many farms and never found dirt. I did, and I am not the only one. Let me quote in my defence the "transplanted Englishwoman." She says—

Even a tent is preferable to close contact with people whose ways in "little things that count" are offensive. The discomforts of a small room, an uneven floor, and an inadequate supply of crockery are discomforts that one can be happy with. The presence of a man who spits on the floor, and of a room-mate who never bathes and cannot stand a breath of fresh air in a fetid sleeping-room, are discomforts which, to a refined woman, mean Purgatory. I speak from a month's experience of this species of discomfort in a backwoods homestead. The bed to which I was introduced had no sheets, and the blankets were of a dirty greyish-brown colour, and had been in use all the winter. There was but one sleeping-place, as it was termed, for the whole family and any chance visitors, flimsy curtains separating the beds. There were, of course, no toilet arrangements. Every one was supposed to wash and comb his or her hair in the kitchen, the small wash-basin and hanging glass having their place on a bench which held the water-pails, saucepans, etc. I caused much amazement by taking the basin of water and my own hair-brush and hand-glass out to the cowshed, and there performing my toilet in a clean corner. The men chewed and spat continuously while indoors.

This is in the nature of corroboration, I think. Then my critic on the Regina paper accuses me of a vulgar offence, one which wounds me even to think of, wholly undeserved as it is. " Accepting hospitality with outward cordiality, feeling wrathful and vicious, and writing up one's host and hostess to expose their faults and failings." I may have drawn this accusation upon myself by not stating in every article that wherever I went through the whole of my journey I said straight off, " I am

writing of things as I find them over here. May I
make notes of your daily doings and surroundings
and use them? Do you mind?" I never went to
any place without making my purpose clear. I
always asked permission. I never took bread and
salt under guise of an ordinary friendly visit. With
the accordance of such permission my way lay clear.
It was always given; if it was given under the idea
that I should smooth the rough and gloss the dull,
then I am sorry—for the giver. The writer says I
felt "wrathful" and vicious. I put it to those who
have read this chapter, Have I seemed vicious?
"Wrathful." Yes. Wrathful with the conditions
of any social system which can breed people in
ignorance and dirt, but the wrath is for England,
the sorrow for Canada that there should be grafted
on to her fine stock such undesirables of our civilization. I have not over-stated one fact in that
article, nothing is set down in malice, bare record is
all I have attempted. Finally I would say that if
the Western paper which quoted my article did not
say it was one of a series, and quote or outline the
others it did me an injustice.

I have refrained from statistics in these prairie
descriptions because I so well remember how they
made the very name of Canada a boredom to me,

before I came over and saw the beautiful country. But some of the officials to whom I betrayed this ill-governed dislike were very shocked. They said no book on the country is any good that does not comment on its marvellous figures; one of them drew up a beautiful table for my private edification. I have not read it. But here it is, lest any fall by the way in learning of Canada from me, and think it is all landscape and no dollars.

WESTERN CROPS, 1909

The following is the *Official Government Estimate* of 1909 crops, dated Ottawa, 15th October, 1909, and covering the Provinces of Manitoba, Saskatchewan and Alberta only—

		Bushels.
Wheat, total yield .	. . .	120,340,000
Oats, ,, ,,	. . .	156,800,000
Barley, ,, ,,	. . .	30,240,000

At their present market values the above crops represent the gigantic sum of nearly $185,000,000.

A FEW COMPARATIVE FACTS

The total gold production from the Yukon for *ten years*, from 1896 to 1906, represents a value of $114,000,000; but, from this year's crop alone, our Western farmers will earn about *sixty-two per cent. more* than the above sum.

The total value of diamonds produced in 1905 (last available figures) from the world's richest mines at Kimberley, South Africa, was about	$34,000,000
The total output of gold for the same year from the entire Transvaal reached the sum of about	$104,000,000
Or taken together	$138,000,000

Our Western farmers will realize a greater sum by about *thirty per cent.* from this season's crop.

The whole world's silver production for the year 1905 totalled a value of $282,000,000. Our Western farmers will earn from this year's crop a sum equal to more than half of the value of the whole world's annual output of silver.

The world's gold production for 1905 totalled about $380,000,000. The earnings of our Western farmers from this year's crops will represent a sum equal to about *forty-nine per cent.* of the value of the whole world's output of gold for the year mentioned.

.　　.　　.　　.　　.　　.

Canada represents about one-third of the entire area of the whole British Empire. Yet, only one-quarter of this area is at present occupied, and only about one-fortieth is under cultivation.

I still like my way best. But that may be obstinacy.

CHAPTER VII

POULTRY FARMING AND MARKET GARDENING

ALTHOUGH I am anxiously looking out for "bachelor" women on the prairies I do not seem to find any. I mean by this phrase women who are working the land "on their own," singly or in clusters. At last it is borne in upon me that there are no women on the prairies except the wives and daughters of farmers, and they are scarce enough; but travelling as I am doing at this stage of my visit, week in and week out, over soil so rich, I am constrained to wonder if there is any reason why women should not come out and work it as well as men. No one questions its fertility and abundant profits, nor the fact that hundreds of healthy Englishwomen are encumbering the old country and leading profitless lives. The labour of "homesteading" would be very great for women, I can understand their shirking it; and the lure of 160 acres of free land is not so golden, when faced in detail, now that Canada is fast settling up, as it is impossible to homestead within easy reach of the railway, a most important matter where the question of carrying goods to market is concerned. The distance, too, doubles the expense of conveying lumber for fuel and building purposes, furniture and implements and stock to the farm; it also makes the homesteader a very lonely person. To "make good" on a free farm a woman would need either much courage and capital, or considerable male labour, besides agricultural skill.

Land, however, can still be bought at any price from ten dollars (£2) an acre and upwards within a few miles of the railway, and only those who have been over here can appreciate the opportunities for money-making in Canada. Women in England have no conception of the openings there are for them in the great North-West. Given health and industry, there is a fortune waiting for them in that marvellous prairie loam, just as surely as for the men who go out to grow wheat and run stock-farms. Above all there is a splendid opening for our women gardeners. Plenty of women now-a-days train in agriculture and horticulture, but the demand for their services is at best small in Great Britain, while it is urgent round the rapidly growing prairie towns. These towns are utterly unlike anything English; built of wood, they spring up like mushrooms wherever some accident of rail or water in the locality makes them convenient centres of access to the outer world. Thither come the farmers and ranchers to sell and buy, to bring their sick, to fetch their mail, to hire the labour which is so dear and scarce in the North-West—and to "see life."

They are excellent centres, moreover, for the sale of market garden produce, which at present is, like labour, both dear and scarce. The Canadian house-wives use tinned goods to a tremendous extent because their men prefer the big gamble of wheat-growing to the steady, if slower, road to fortune offered by vegetable, fruit and flower growing. Here, then, is the opportunity for Englishwomen. Let them come out in twos and threes, unless any single woman has herself sufficient capital, and (just as important) courage for a lonely life; let them settle within marketable driving distance of such cities as Saskatoon, Regina, Edmonton, Calgary, etc., and they will find awaiting them every facility for a life of independence and certain ultimate success in the grandest climate in the world. The brilliant bracing air, the bustle of industry and of hope which pervade the prairies are beyond my powers to describe. If they would prefer to try such a centre as Winnipeg they must be prepared to pay bigger prices for their land, or else to settle near the smaller towns, like Birtle, which is eight hours by rail from Winnipeg, where excellent land is to be bought for ten dollars (£2) an acre. Mr. Larcombe has 800 acres at Birtle, where he raises excellent wheat, yet he finds it pays him to devote more and more of his land every year to growing potatoes, beets, tomatoes, pumpkins, etc., for the Winnipeg market. He would be an invaluable and willing adviser to any one proposing to compete with him; it sounds altruistic, but the market is large and grows yearly larger; also he is an ardent Imperialist who keenly desires to see British settlers on Canadian soil. It is possible to settle within an hour, by electric car, from the city on the Assiniboine River, but land there fetches 250 dollars an acre. Winnipeg offers a greater market for fruit, flowers and vegetables than any city in Canada. It imports hundreds of car-loads yearly from the United States, all subject to 33 per cent. duty, not to mention the high freight rates. The soil is magnificent, a warm quick vegetable mould which has been known to produce 650 bushels of potatoes to the acre. Figuring that out at 50 cents a bushel shows a yield of 325 dollars an acre, and 50 cents is a low estimate. I met a man here in September who had just received 1.25 to 1.50 dollars per bushel for his last load!

All vegetables sell readily. Some of the companies will do the first year's ploughing for buyers of market garden lots, and take payment by instalment as profits come along; personally I should always suggest the advisability of starting fair with sufficient capital to be unencumbered by any such debt, although many a wealthy Canadian of to-day began in that way.

Land round the other cities I mentioned can be purchased now for twenty-five dollars to thirty dollars an acre, generally speaking, and they offer a steadily growing market. Round Saskatoon land may be bought for anything from ten dollars to twenty-five dollars an acre, in accordance with its proximity to the city, a factor the value of which to a market gardener it is unnecessary to emphasize. The soil is of marvellous fertility—three to four feet of loam over clay—and one or two of the townspeople have begun to grow their own vegetables, in despair of getting them any other way. In Mrs. Hanson's garden at Saskatoon are cucumbers, carrots, tomatoes, marrows, asparagus, celery, onions, beets, radishes, turnips, potatoes, strawberries, raspberries, currants and gooseberries. The season is short, and housekeepers who can get fresh vegetables store them in "root-cellars" for the winter—they are also very clever at pickling them. As evidence of the rapid growth of these prairie cities I may mention that Saskatoon had 200 inhabitants six years ago, and has 10,000 to-day. The story of the transformation of Winnipeg I have already narrated. Edmonton is one of the most beautiful and prosperous of the prairie cities—and Calgary, "the capital of ranchland," is another wonderful place for such a venture as I am advocating. It stands at the feet of the Rocky Mountains, is warmed throughout the winter by Chinook winds, fed by a glacial river of indescribable beauty, and boasts, even in Canada, an atmosphere of exceptional brilliance and exhilaration.

For the benefit of such of its subjects as live by the soil, the Dominion Government, as I have already said, supports nine experimental farms, of which two are in Saskatchewan, two in Alberta, and one in Manitoba, so that the prairie provinces are well supplied. The importance of these farms to settlers is beyond count—there experiments are ceaselessly in progress for the identification and destruction of weeds and pests, for the breeding out of flowers, fruit, grain and vegetables which will stand the hard North-West winters, or ripen before the earliest frost, or in some way render the grower immune from climatic hazards in his ventures. The farms exist solely for the use of the people, and results of successful experiments are made public property at once; advice is given free, and the literature they publish is of extraordinary value to those interested in the land. I have spoken of these farms before, but the matter will bear repetition in connection with market gardening.

I am particularly struck with the possibilities for women market gardeners at the Manitoba Hall in Winnipeg, where I am in time to see the Horticultural Exhibition. There I find an old familiar friend, Beauty of Hebron, and Early Rose, and Early Jersey Wakefield, among other potato tribes. The latter were sown on June 17th, and win first prize on September 1st. Strange pear-shaped tomatoes, too, I see; Swiss Chard, an unfamiliar vegetable, with stalks like flat white rhubarb ending in a leaf similar to that of a cabbage with white veins; petunias, asters, carnations, zinnias, stocks, sweet peas, cacti and a few pathetic half-wild roses. Pumpkins and citrons are here, and home-made wines and jams in abundance—yellow misty dandelion wine that carries me back to thirsty childhood hours in the hay-fields, when sunburnt peasants drank dandelion "beer" out of big stone bottles, and we children clamoured vainly for that nectar instead of tepid milk. One never-to-be-forgótten day I persuaded an infant brother to accompany me to the stone jar, and we drank furtively, like the dwarfs in the old myth, of that Odhærir, honey-sweet and just as fatal, for the Odin-eye of a parent discovered us later disgracefully fuddled under a briar hedge. I am straying from my subject, however, and will not pursue the story; it is hardly a creditable one, and nothing whatever to do with Canada; moreover, the rest of it is painful even in remembrance. To return to Manitoba Hall, I see parsnip wine, bronze like an Austrian copper briar rose with the sun on it; cherry wine, black and opaque; white currant, a warm orange; raspberry vinegar, homely pickles; and one exhibit round which I hover fascinated—the sweet herbs! Thyme, summer savory, sage, marjoram with flowers like "cherry pie" or heliotrope, and sweet basil, with its pale green spikes and small white flowers, indissolubly connected with memories of Keats and Isabella.

Herbs are always quaintly attractive with their beautiful names, their odd perfumes, their virtues and sobriety. English cooks ignore them in the most unintelligent fashion, few will use rosemary for veal stuffing, or put chervil, tarragon or dande-

lion into their lettuce salads, thereby missing countless subtleties dear to a discriminating palate. Mint
and parsley they will admit in their dishes, but the
difficulty of getting an English cook to put a
chopped chive-spike with mashed potatoes is beyond
belief—sometimes they will rise to borage for Cup,
but chives for potatoes—never. As Schloesser has
it, "once upon a time, when things went more slowly
and life was easier, the culture and culling of the
simples which went to make the olitory, or herb
garden, was as much a part of female education as a
nice deportment." It is with considerable admiration, therefore, that I linger by the herb stall in Manitoba Hall and see that Canadians are not above
growing herbs. There is an immense market for
market garden produce out West—flowers are dear
and sell well; vegetables are greatly needed; it
seems an infinite pity, therefore, that any one should
think of inserting such an advertisement as appeared the other day in a Surrey paper. A trained
woman gardener offered her services free in ex-
change for a house! It sounds incredible; but it
is a fact. Nor is it unusual in England. Here is a
woman, trained expensively, ready to haggle her
skill for a home! Why does she not go out West,
where many a farmer would gladly pay her well to

"run" a few acres for flowers and vegetables, while he and his men attend to the wheat growing? She can save money and ultimately buy her own land; it is easy to save in these wild places of the world, where there are none of the lures to spend which make saving such a dire and difficult game in the old country; there are no after-season sales, no entertaining, no taxicabs, no theatres; it is hard to spend money indeed; and there is every inducement to make it. It is easy to acquire land in a slow, sane, industrious way, and work it profitably. Market gardening requires no such outlay as wheat farming; that is a venture which does not begin to pay till 160 acres are tilled, a feat which takes some doing in the bush-covered parts of the prairie with only a scrub-plough to help. The ploughing of a few acres, on the other hand, is not a very formidable undertaking, and returns in flowers and vegetables would be steady.

Before I left England a woman I know asked me to look out for an opening for her out West. Her comely face, drawn into puckers of anxiety, haunts me as I travel; I make inquiries on her behalf, and get five offers for her services on the prairie lands, one in Nova Scotia, none in British Columbia. Four out of the five would-be employers are anxious to engage her as domestic help, practically as servant, a post at which I beg no reader to sniff. Every woman is a servant where labour is so scarce, and the wives among them throw in their travail and child-rearing as well! The wages offered range from ten to twenty dollars a month. The fifth offer is to run a poultry department on a large farm of 800 acres near Winnipeg. The farmer wants to keep poultry, there is a good market for it in the city; his daughters are already fully occupied with the housework and dairy, and he would like an Englishwoman "for company" for them as well as to manage the poultry. He says he will "deed" her five acres to work on, make them wolf-proof, although he cannot promise they will be hawk-proof, and give her fifteen dollars a month, to become twenty if she likes the work and stays on, and as perquisite all the eggs to sell that are not wanted for the house or for sitting. I remember the worried face in the Devonshire rose-garden—

"Auntie is very kind, but what am I to do when she dies? I have no trade; I look after the fowls for her; she gives me five shillings a week for that, and I have to dress on it. I can't save. I am thirty. I shall never marry now. No one wants an old maid. . . ." I remember her, and tell the farmer I think I know an Englishwoman who will suit. I picture her round, rosy, good-tempered chubbiness in this land barren of women, and tell myself that some lonely farmer will learn one day how clever she is in all female arts, sewing, cooking and filling a house brimful of domestic comforts, and I write to her detailing all the offers, keeping the best till the last; but she does not come.

What is the fatal inertia which makes our women remain parasites on the community? Do they fear to travel? Why do they persist in staying in a country where they are not wanted, just because they were born in it?

I never learn why the Devonshire girl goes on living with an aunt who thinks herself a philanthropist for keeping here. The only reason ever offered is, "It seems such a dreadful long way away from every one."

Hawks and wolves on the prairie do much damage among the poultry, I gather. The "boys" shoot the hawks and trap the wolves, but they are very tiresome. The prairie wolf must not be confounded with the savage timber wolf, and is more properly known as a coyote; he is more like a wild dog, and is occasionally dangerous when driven by hunger and hunting in large packs—never when by himself.

The coyotes howl in shrill intermittent style, eerie
and discordant. They are commonly called wolves
among the settlers, and their coats make excellent
rugs for the sleighs in winter. A coyote is responsible on one occasion for a paroxysm of homesickness
on my part! I am being entertained to tea at a
farmhouse and presently mother has to clear up and
put a brace of babes to bed, so Miss Seven-year-old
takes me for a walk round the byres. I try to tell
her about the King of the Swallows, who pulls the
hair off the reels in little girls' heads and makes it
grow long, awfully long, but she muddles him up
with Absalom; a similar fate overtakes Cinderella,
who, by some obscure mental process, she confounds
with Daniel in the lions' den; thus we drift into
Sunday school talk, and I learn a lot. She has a
lovely face, this little prairie girl, with a pale, fine
skin and wide blue eyes, deep, dark blue, fringed
with black lashes. She is very animated. I am hearing about "Amananeve" and a serpent, when a long
wild keening rends the air. Upon a mound near by
a coyote points his nose to the sky. Her chatter
ceases, and she clings to me trembling: "I don't
like the wolves." Whereupon memory plays me a
cruel trick; I feel as if it were my own little chatter-
box clinging to me, and I want to leave Canada and

all it contains and rush to her. We retire indoors discomfited, and, to cheer Miss Seven-year-old, I sing Moody and Sankey hymns to the harmonium while the rig is being got ready to take me away. It is the only music I can find.

I learn a great deal about poultry farming from Mr. Prain, of the Scottish Agricultural Commission, during my sojourn in Edmonton. He is one of the greatest living authorities on poultry, and does not keep all his knowledge to himself like some experts. If it is not an impertinence I should like to say in passing that the report of that Commission should be of inestimable value to any intending emigrant to Canada. It contains the collected opinions of twenty-two Scotchmen, men of repute, position and learning, all experts in agricultural matters, who went through Canada last autumn at the behest of the Dominion Government to report on the conditions of the country and the possibilities it offers to settlers. It is published by Blackwood and Sons at the modest sum of one shilling; here is part of Mr. Prain's report on poultry keeping, a branch of farming which Englishwomen with some capital and a desire for a career would do well to study—

POULTRY FARMING

Canada possesses unique opportunities for raising poultry keeping to an important industry. With the exception of the bare prairie lands, there is abundant natural shelter everywhere in the woods, forest, and bushy scrub which clothe the earth, providing not only protection from the weather, but affording a supply of insect and animal food so necessary to the health of this kind of stock. In the apple orchards of the eastern provinces, in British Columbia, and in the magnificent fruit valley of the Niagara Peninsula, no better conditions could exist for the profitable keeping of fowls; the two industries of fruit growing and poultry keeping so naturally fit into and supplement each other. Whilst the fruit-trees supply the shade from the sun and the shelter from the storm, so helpful and beneficial to the fowls, these active, foraging animals are continually devouring all insect and grub pests which are their natural food, but which are the deadly enemies of the fruit-trees. Then the labour connected with the two industries is so divided that the busy season of the fruit picking is distinctly separated from the hatching and rearing of the chickens. Particularly is the labour reduced when the birds are put out in colony houses all over the orchards. The minimum of attention is required by this system, while the ground derives the benefit from the manure being equally distributed over it. There is ample evidence of the successful combination of these two industries, to the mutual benefit of both, to prove that this practice might be most judiciously and profitably extended.

The prices obtained for table poultry and eggs all over Canada assure a profit to the producer under good management. Taking the whole country, the lowest summer price for eggs will not be under 8*d*. per dozen, and the minimum winter price not under 1*s*. 5*d*. per dozen. Table chickens bring 8*d*. per lb., dressed weight, rising to 1*s*. per lb. for crate-fattened birds. Ducklings make about the same rates, and there is always a good market for turkeys and geese. In British Columbia prices are much higher, but this is counteracted to some extent by the dearer price of poultry food. In the eastern provinces grain is also somewhat high in price, but with better distributing facilities from the great grain-growing areas, prices will gradually be equalized. Cheap frosted wheat is often available, and this can be used freely along with other kinds of food. Although the past six or seven years have seen an enormous increase in the poultry produce of the Dominion, prices, in sympathy with the other markets of the world, are tending upwards.

From the last census returns of 1901 the total poultry population of Canada is stated at 17,922,658. Competent authorities estimate that the province of Ontario alone now possesses 13,000,000 hens, so that in 1908 the poultry population was probably twice what it was in 1901. Yet in spite of this doubled working plant, as it might be called, the consuming capacity of the Dominion has been increasing at a higher ratio. While at one time it was considered impossible to consume all the produce raised, it has now become the problem to supply the home market. In 1902, 11,635,108 dozens of eggs were exported, valued at 1,733,242 dollars. This had fallen in 1906 to 2,921,725 dozens, valued at 495,176 dollars, and in 1908 to 1,365,890 dozens, valued at 301,818 dollars. From 1902 to 1906 the value of imported eggs had fallen from 169,457 dollars to 88,937 dollars. In 1908 the value of the imports of eggs was 214,994 dollars. The fall in exports, especially to Britain, is due to the increased demands of the home market. This strong local demand is an undoubted incentive to greater effort on the part of the Canadian poultry grower. The exports and imports of live birds have both notably increased, due presumably to the freer interchange of breeding stock between Canada and other countries. Very few large utility or commercial poultry farms are to be found in Canada. The tendency is rather to extend the industry on surer and better lines through the farmers taking a more intelligent interest in the fowls, and making them a regular paying part of the farm stock.

The exhibition side of poultry keeping is well advanced in Canada. Fanciers are numerous, and as keenly active in introducing and improving new breeds as they are in the old country. They play their part in fostering and educating public opinion. They also distribute eggs and cockerels of pure breeds, which go to build up and improve the strains of other breeders. Conversation with many of these fanciers brought out that the demand for pure eggs and cockerels of the useful varieties was increasing enormously, indirectly proving the greater interest manifested in poultry keeping. At most of the agricultural shows exhibitions of poultry stock are encouraged by liberal classification and good prizes. Table poultry and egg classes are almost invariably provided.

In the maritime provinces of Prince Edward Island, Nova Scotia and New Brunswick the opportunities for successful poultry keeping are to some slight extent modified by the price of grain, which has to be carried for food to all kinds of stock from the Far West. The heavy carriage, with the dealer's and speculator's profit added, makes dear grain, thus raising the cost of production. At the same time a flock of fowls, from twenty-five to a hundred or so on each farm, when looked after with reasonable care, leaves a good margin of profit. The waste grain, vegetables, etc., augmented by a small quantity of maize meal, carries the birds through the winter at a very small cost. Farmers generally are doing well with their fowls, and the custom of adding these to the regular stock of the farm is rapidly increasing. . . .

Quebec and Ontario, being the oldest settled provinces, with several large cities as convenient markets, naturally take the lead in the production of poultry produce. From these provinces a considerable surplus is sent west every year to the growing towns, the mining districts, and British Columbia. Poultry keeping is much more recognized as a regular part of the *régime* of the farm in these provinces than it is anywhere else in the Dominion. With the MacDonald College near Montreal, the Central Experimental Farm at Ottawa, the Ontario College at Guelph, the scientific and educative sides of poultry keeping are well provided for. The wonder is that an organized system of marketing the produce has not yet been introduced. . . .

The provinces of Manitoba, Saskatchewan and Alberta, particularly the latter two, are so much taken up with grain growing, the farms are still so scattered, and labour so difficult to obtain, that no great output of poultry produce can as yet be reasonably looked for. As it is, considerable importations of poultry produce have to be made every year, though this will very soon be reversed when these provinces get more thickly settled. The climate, though sometimes extremely cold in winter, need be no hindrance to the development of the industry.

Many successful examples could be quoted to prove this point. Even round the outskirts of the towns many well-bred flocks of fowls can be seen on the town lots. This might be called a characteristic feature of most Canadian towns, the birds being kept more with an eye to profit than merely as a hobby. Turkeys seem to thrive so well in these provinces that it might be profitable to specialize in the production of this favourite table delicacy. . . . In Alberta in 1906 the Provincial Government started co-operative poultry fattening stations at five centres, Wetaskawin, Lacombe, Red Deer, Innisfail, and Olds. The principle of these stations was to take the ordinary unfattened fowls from the farmers, and to fatten, kill, dress and market them. Formerly the farmers only got from eight to ten cents per pound live weight, then crate-fattened, killed, dressed and put them on the market. After deducting all costs the farmers were returned four and a quarter cents per pound, in addition to the eight cents advanced at purchase. This system had been successfully established in other districts. Alberta has now engaged an expert to devote his whole time to the development of poultry keeping in the province. Throughout the whole of the north-west provinces poultry stock keep remarkably healthy. The wet weather in the hatching season, particularly in June, is probably the worst handicap the farmers have to contend with, but this might probably be obviated by earlier hatching and by a little more attention to housing.

In British Columbia the opportunities for poultry keeping are most inviting. In fact, almost ideal conditions exist for this industry in the fine climate, associated often with excellent soil and unlimited shelter. When to these natural advantages is added a splendid home market for the produce in the mining districts and in Vancouver, the wonder is that much more is not done in this direction. As in Nova Scotia, the fruit orchards might most judiciously be more extensively used as chicken nurseries. Feed is certainly higher, but this only relates to grains, and after all, fowls in such conditions as usually predominate in British Columbia can be kept at a moderate cost. At Agassiz Experimental Farm there is a poultry branch which distributes a considerable number of eggs and cockerels. In Vancouver Island, where fruit growing and market gardening are extensively gone into, it is the custom to keep flocks of fowls in conjunction with these two industries. The Okanagan Valley, and other districts of the same kind, present most favourable opportunities for the development of this industry. Looking at all the circumstances, there seems no reason why British Columbia should not supply her own markets with poultry produce, as well as export a surplus, rather than have to import it as at present.

The united testimony gathered from all experimental farms, and other reliable sources, agrees in the essential principles of housing. It must be borne in mind that the winter over the greater part of Canada lasts at least four months, and that the temperature falls occasionally to forty and forty-five degrees below zero, while the thermometer often registers one hundred degrees in summer. The variations of temperature are accordingly much greater than in Britain. The housing problem is, therefore, one of the utmost importance. One of the recognized essentials, then, is light; at least one-third part of the south, or front end of the house, should be of glass or open to the sun.

Abundance of fresh air is of equal importance; this is secured by having the front of the house almost entirely open, but protected in extreme weather by cotton curtains or sliding glass windows. The open front, with sides, back and roof tight, gives plenty of fresh air without draught or through ventilation. The minimum depth of a house of this kind should not be under eight feet, with the perches low and close to the back. An additional cotton screen suspended before the perches when the weather becomes extreme, protects the combs and feet of the birds from being frozen. In some houses with span roofs the upper space is packed with straw, which admits of top-ventilation and absorbs moisture as well; but, with the proper amount of open front, the straw is unnecessary. The main idea is perfect dryness of atmosphere inside the house. Dampness to any degree is fatal with low temperatures, therefore the floor ought to be tightly jointed and raised from the ground six or eight inches, as well as littered three or four inches deep with cut straw or roughage of some kind. It is marvellous how birds thrive and lay in the coldest weather when housed as above described.

POULTRY FARMING

The tendency at the present time is to feed dry grain and discontinue mash foods. It is admitted that mash foods may force growth in the young birds, and also stimulate egg production, but for breeding stock the eggs are considered to hatch better and give stronger chicks when dry food is used. Sometimes sprouted grain, or grain steeped in boiling water, is given, also clover leaves or cut clover which has been well steeped in boiling water. Green food, such as mangels, turnips, cabbage and sugar beets, is freely fed, also animal meal or green bone. The self-feeding hopper system is quite commonly adopted for grain, bran, etc., and also for oyster-shell and grit. Where wet mash food is used the practice is tending towards giving it at night instead of in the morning. The custom of scattering grain in the litter is universal, and altogether the methods of feeding seem to be most intelligently understood. . . .

The tendency of the Canadian farmer is to go in for general purpose fowls, rather than for those with pronounced characteristics of one kind or another. Thus Plymouth Rocks, Wyandottes, Orpingtons and Rhode Island Reds may be reckoned the favourites, with Plymouth

M   177

Rocks easily leading. This variety is undoubtedly the standard fowl of the country, and it certainly seems to fulfil its dual purpose of egg production and table qualities admirably. Some strains, such as those at Guelph Experimental Farm, are remarkable for their prolific laying, early maturity and fine table qualities. The White Wyandotte and Buff Orpington are also much kept for their all-round good points, while the Rhode Island Reds are considered extremely hardy. Of the Mediterranean breeds, probably the Brown and White Leghorns are the most popular, with Minorcas and Andalusians next.

CHAPTER VIII

FROM Edmonton to Calgary. The pulses dance to think of it, for that means a journey afterwards through the Rocky Mountains, the wonderful, the world-famed! Before I leave the prairie city, however, which to me must ever be connected with pictures of the Agricultural Commission and long talks on poultry, I meet Mrs. Balmer Watt, an interesting journalist, whose little book *Town and Trail* is very well worth reading by any woman who thinks of settling in Edmonton. The Press all over Canada has been very good to me; here and now I would like to tender it my heartiest thanks. Mrs. Balmer Watt has been caught by the spirit of the West, the bias of her mind leads her to analyze and brood over it, unlike the majority who merely take it for granted and enjoy it. "Out on the prairies," she says, "face to face with their naked souls, men and women come into possession of a depth of wisdom impossible to attain surrounded by the distractions of the town. And what, after all, is the secret of the spirit that animates the whole West . . . from the centre of the newest cities to the uttermost ends of the farthest distant homesteads . . . but the joy of labour, the satisfaction of knowing in each man's hands lies the possibility of his own future?" True words.

I leave Edmonton, the beautiful, prosperous capital of Alberta, built on the banks of a gold-bearing river, and storm Calgary in a mazy hurry to see Mr. Turner's ranch; he is out of town, so I miss the ranch, but am entertained delightfully by the editor of the *Calgary Herald*, with whose wife I have a long talk about the need of maternity nurses on the prairie. More of that later. And then Calgary, the capital of Ranchland, the gate to the Rocky Mountains—happy Calgary nestling in the beautiful cup that is neither prairie nor mountain, but girt with both—Calgary moves away from the train, and I watch her fade into distance; we are approaching the great gate of the mountains which stretches between the prairies and the Pacific slopes. Travellers tell of it, how it towers to heaven and leans to hell, how it is riven of valleys and gives back sound with a terrible voice, how it is ranged by the bear and shadowed by the lone eagle. Men with pens dipped in fire have told of the Rockies, I will be betrayed into no competition with them. The air that sweeps

by is brilliant and rare, so rare that it makes a novice
"out of breath," but it gives at the same time a tremendous exhilaration of spirits. That phrase comes
old and stale, it sounds like the sort of thing everybody will say who speaks of mountains, but it means
a very great deal, it means that one is happy—and
happiness is the gift of the gods, sought desperately
all the world over, from the loafer in a gin-palace
to the King watching his horse win the Derby. I
lean from the end of the car, and the silver rails slip
away from our wheels. As we approach the greatest
scenic track of railway in the world a fellow-traveller
tells of the old days of the road when men fed on
fishy pork—pork which in its lifetime had wandered
by the shore eating dead salmon—the days when
they shot for the pot and not for sport, when they
lived for a week on a trumpeter swan and fed on
white beans for a fortnight. Here is the perfected
result of those days of travail for all the world to
enjoy. As the train enters the Bow River Valley
and the mountains close in upon us, I learn the taste
of awe.

Under Mount Stephen stands a brown house built
of wooden shingles, in the hall is a great open hearth
where logs burn continuously. Here the sportsmen
come and go—go in a flurry of earnest hope, and

return excited or depressed as they have found the sport, though they never come back empty-handed. If they have not grizzly bear they have black bear, if not caribou they have deer. Standing by the dancing logs I watch the last bear-parties come in from Leanchoil, very happy and excited, with three splendid skins; a slight fair woman who has been standing near the fire too, for the first snow has fallen, goes up to them and talks about their sport. Presently one of them calls her by name, "Mrs. Schäffer"; I look at her with intense interest, there could hardly be two women of that name in this particular spot. It is known to every one that she started from here in June intending to go over the Wilcox Pass, down the Athabasca, and up the Miette River, across the Yellowhead to the old Tête Jaune Cache. Every one has heard how she started on horseback with one other woman, two guides and a pack-train of twenty-two horses. There can hardly be two Mrs. Schäffers, I tell myself, at this place in September. I study her closely; she has fair hair that has been burned fairer by the sun, a skin once fair, now deeply tanned, slim arms that are browner still, and a smooth voice with a strong American accent. What can this little woman have in her so fearless that she is gaining the reputation of an intrepid explorer? Her manner is gentle; one derides the notion of a bias to masculinity; perhaps she is so sincerely an artist that she loves the virgin wild before its bloom is pushed aside by the white man's presence, for the red man defiles no more than the caribou or wandering bear. If this is the Mrs. Schäffer I mean, she is the woman who lectures before geographical societies, who illustrated with her brush the *Alpine Flora of the Canadian Rockies*, who has written for the *Canadian Alpine Journal* and the *Geographical Journal of Philadelphia*, and who lectured in Boston before the Appalachian Club; the woman who goes on exploring expeditions for three or four months at a time—and who is mentioned by Kipling in his *Letters*.

Later in the day we meet and talk, and I see the companion of her travels for the last three expeditions, Miss Adams, a little dark, neat woman and a keen geologist, with a head shaped beautifully like that of an Egyptian priest. They talk amusingly, and without the least pride, of their "trip," they show me countless photographs taken on the way. "First you must meet Mr. Muggins. He is the dearest. See his sad face, he got to thinking us a parcel of lunatics at times when we kept him too long on the raft. Oh! and you *must* see the raft, it was the most primitive thing, but we were so proud of it. When we found the horses could not swim the Maligne we 'unpacked' them and got across on the raft, it was the only way. Another time we had to unpack them and coax them one by one over a twenty-foot bluff with a rope. I say 'we' did, but really our two guides did; they are both Englishmen, and nobody can imagine the care and trouble those two men took! The passing of that bluff is becoming history in the country. It was always supposed to be impassable. I am afraid the photograph is rather indistinct."

It is rather, but I manage to make out the figure of a perturbed horse coming down a precipice at an acute angle, and a row of others looking nervously on from above.

"Here is our camp on the Maligne Lake. We had great trouble in finding that lake. We got there eventually from a map drawn by Sampson Beaver, one of the Stony Tribe, an Indian who had never seen a map in his life. It was the crudest pencil sketch in the world, but it served its purpose. It is twenty miles long, and has never known a sound save the moccasined foot of the Indians. Ours was the first white man's camp in that far-away hunting ground. Here is our pack-train—yes, the figure on

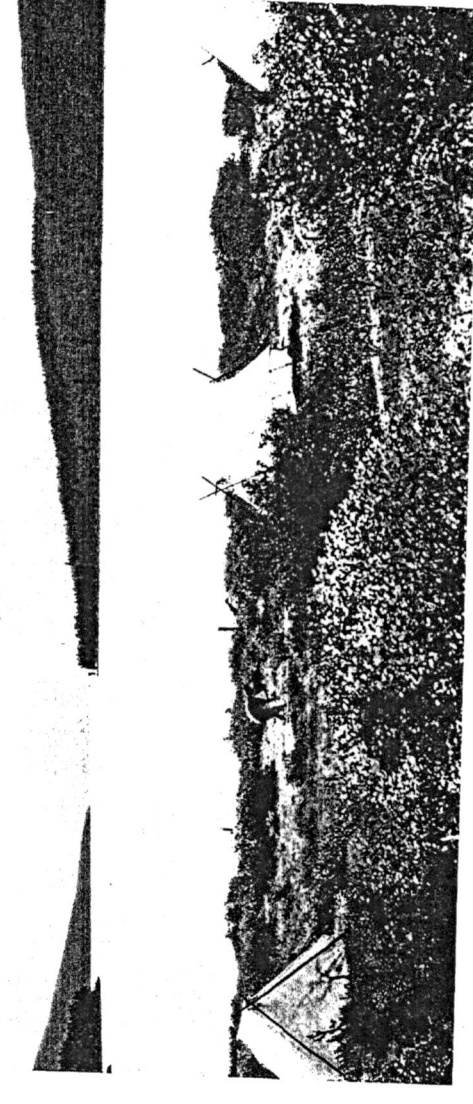

horseback is me—we both wore breeches in the wild, it's safer, skirts are a concession to civilization. Say, isn't this child cute? Her mother is a quarter-breed and her father a white man, yet look at the Indian in that child! See the way she carries her doll. And she brought it in a moss-bag! Here is a tiny picture of the raft going over the lake; do look at Mr. Muggins being carried over the Saskatchewan, he is very amusing when the water is at all rough. He just sits and cries till he is carried, and when he is safe in his master's arms he looks as proud and indifferent as possible. Here is our dinner-table. You see it shows five diners, and obviously another present to take the photograph. That comes about because the first month we had Mr. Brown the botanist and his guide with us. After that we were only the four. Here is Mount Robson, the highest mountain in the Rocky range, and at the most only photographed twice before."

"What made you begin?" I ask.

"Well!—I began with the botanical work, making small explorations in search of plants. In that way I learned to live on horseback, to camp out two days, four days, a week, two weeks, a month, four months, and so on; to jump muskegs, to take a loaded animal up and round rock ridges, to keep a foothold on slippery, sliding mud. After I had learned so much it was hard to sit with folded hands listening politely to the stories of Colin, Stutfield, Wooley, Outram, Fay, Thompson and Coleman of the hills I so longed to see—stories of the vast unexplored glorious country *beyond!* It bred rebellion. We looked to each other and said, 'Why not? We can starve as well as they; a muskeg will be no softer for us than for them, the ground will be no harder to sleep on, the waters no deeper to swim nor colder if we fall in.'"

So they talk; telling vivaciously, without vanity, of their amazing venture; giving photographs, some of which appear in this chapter. The "muskeg" referred to is bogland; it is the word used over here for dangerous, treacherous bogs which seem to abound both in the Rockies and Ontario. (I am liable to remember the Ontarian belt as I was caught in the Kenora washout, where a cloud-burst washed away a long stretch of track built over difficult boggy land, and my train was thirty hours late arriving at Winnipeg!) I met Miss Agnes Laut, the authoress; I go to Emerald Lake and wonder, as every traveller wonders, at the deep green waters, clear and brilliant, cradled among the mountains, with no apparent excuse for their wonderful colour. The châlet is empty, it is late in the year for travellers, but the man in charge comes out to see how we are impressed with his beautiful lake. Directly he speaks I know him for English—he is a Birmingham man. We chat a little, he is of the rover type and loves the wild mountain fastnesses. We mention New Street, the Arcade, Five Ways, Hagley Road—each name painting a different picture of the busy Midland metropolis to our English minds—the words strike crudely on the ear by the calm waterside, they echo incongruously up the steeps, though we speak softly —he takes his pipe out of his mouth and looks across the green water—looks at the jagged heights about him, looks to the sunset and grows silent. He would not go back. He could not. If he did the mountains would call till his heart broke. Returning to Mount Stephen, Otto the guide shows me how to " shy " straight. He sees a spruce-partridge on a bough and kills it with a stone. I am impressed less with his skill than with the instinct to kill which animates all his conversation, and is after all his means of livelihood. He tells me that the spruce-partridge is usually known as the fool-hen because of its silly habit of sitting still to be stoned, also that the ruffed willow-grouse is protected by law. He has lived at Leanchoil and Field for seven years, and knows all the trails for two hundred miles round.

I ask if one can fish much here, and he tells tales of the trout in the Kootenays, of the silver and grey heckle, of fishing up to ice-time till my ears ache to hear the keen swish of a line cleaving the air, my eyes to see a silver fly tip the water. Next day I find the west-bound train is cancelled, so start forth to try riding astride; the indescribable mosses, the trees gnawed by porcupine, the thickets bright with scarlet bunch-berries lure one to brave the passes; I find a beast which proves a very Samson among gees; after two or three hours he makes for home just as violently as he started away from it; he has galloped and curveted up the Yoho Pass in great good humour, utterly regardless of the tremors which might possibly possess a rider unused to Rocky Mountain roads. I am wondering if there is any chance of slipping into the hotel unseen— there are no side-saddles "out West." Walking feels odd in this kit. Other women can look very smart and workman-like in the queer Mexican saddles, and out of them too, but I haven't yet "got the habit." Round the last perilous corner, past the livery barn, and over the shining railway track we dash to the hotel steps. I peer about me in the dusky light and cautiously prepare to dismount. No one who has not been in one knows how many humps there are on these Western saddles. I am swaying and struggling in great disturbance of mind when a civil voice offers help.

A lady of apparently forty or so, with one of those even voices that go with "decided" opinions, has seen my difficulties. I explain my modest apprehensions, and she tells me she has felt the same, also that she has been up the Burgess Pass alone and is only just down. I am engineered over the humps and out of the funny wooden stirrups, and I thank her with great respect. Fancy climbing the Burgess alone! The Yoho with a horse is bad enough.

We meet at breakfast next morning and I find she is a very handsome girl of twenty-seven or thereabouts, brilliant in conversation, intelligently vague in all her opinions. It is impossible to *think* and be "decided" since the discovery of radium. There are some buckwheat cakes on the menu, and we have two helpings, then tell each other we are greedy.

"But all nice things are greedy," she says, "babies, you know, and dogs and roses."

I tell her of my vain efforts to grow roses on the sand in Surrey; she tells me to try basic slag, and we wander into a highly technical discourse on rose manners, on habits and varieties, winding up with Mendelian theories.

"I am taking home some seeds of the wild prairie-roses," I tell her, "to try and breed out a garden variety that will stand hard winters."

"So am I," she cries.

We stare, then laugh. Here we are, two lone Englishwomen who have drifted together for an instant in the toil of travel, and a chance word reveals us both bent on the same quest, infinitely interested in the same problems.

She has some relatives lately settled in British Columbia, and has heard so much talk of Canada that she has come out to see for herself if she would like to live in it. She has trained as a horticulturalist, and asks what chances there are for women out here.

"Endless ones for the right kind," I answer warmly. "England is glutted with female labour, Canada faints for want of it. It looks like the simplest problem in the world to solve. In reality it is bristling with difficulties."

Her clever face crinkles into lines of perplexity. "How?" she asks.

"Because Englishwomen are used to a communal life. That's why," I answer.

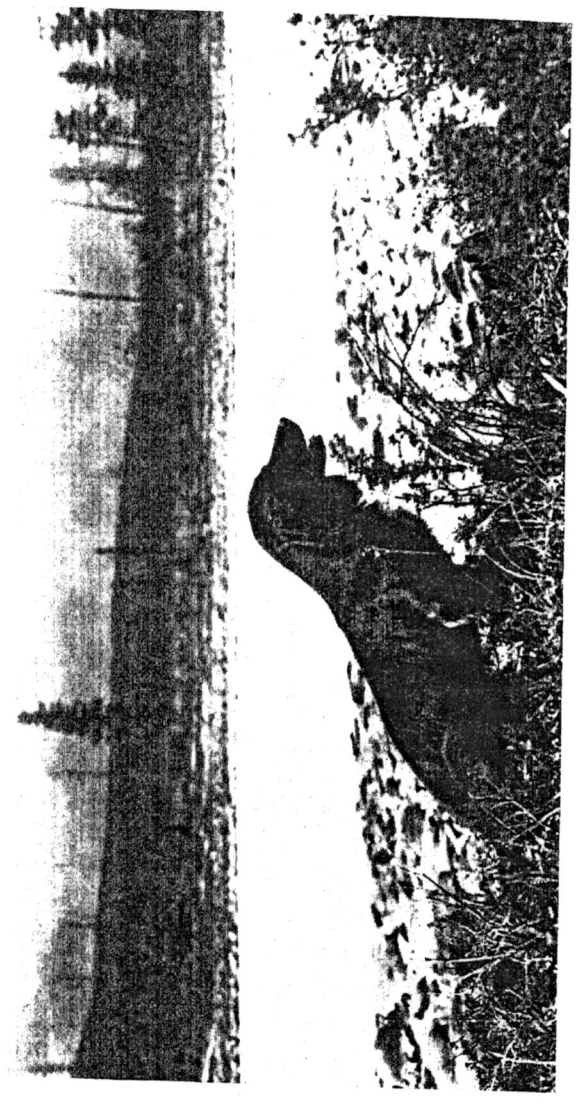

She muses, and I watch her strong, fine face with interest and pleasure. She seems to me to be the embodiment of the best kind of Englishwoman, the kind so greatly needed out West. There is courage in her and endurance, gentleness and refinement too, and all these qualities are lit by the radiant intelligence that beams from every glance.

"You are sure to stay at Victoria later on," she says. "Will you ring me up and tell me if you have time and inclination to stay a few days with me out on the farm?"

We say good-bye. I see her embark on the westbound train with regret—another of the "ships that pass in the night."

Though there are so many English in British Columbia, I seem to become engaged in more of the England v. Canada quarrels there than in any other province in the Dominion; one Mr. Hamber in particular I remember says that the English population of the North-West is greater than in any other part of Canada, and is mostly composed of wastrels—a statement which rouses me to fiery debate. We end in mutual hatred, and I repeat the performance with so many worthy British Columbians that at last big Jim Macdonell proclaims himself my champion. Any one who quarrels with me must fight him—and thereafter peace. "Big Jim" is the biggest man I have ever seen in my life, a Scotchman and a famous engineer. He is doing a tunnelling operation between Laggan and Field for the Canadian Pacific Railway, and has a great colony of navvies encamped like a city for the last two years on the base of operations; he has built a house there for his wife and babies and partner, has a hospital with a doctor and nurse for the staff, and reigns like a burly blue-eyed Scottish chieftain among his men. He tells me a retort to silence the Eastern Canadian with when he quarrels with me about the silliness of English settlers, and he, "Big Jim," is not at hand to fight him—I am to say, "The Englishman in Ontario is a fool? Well, if *you* went West would you know how to throw the diamond hitch?" And they never know. There is only one way to throw the hitch which will fix the pack on a pony's back; an intricate piece of Western lore it is, and quite unknown of the tenderfoot.

I learn a great deal in the mountains about the minerals in this province; there is an aerial lead and silver mine on Mount Stephen, and much talk of ore goes on; I learn that the yield shows about twelve per cent. of zinc, three ounces silver to the ton, and that the only foreign element is lime, the easiest substance

of all to eliminate. I look at it, on the face of the
mountain like Dracula, and can perceive the advantage of its position; it is above the railway, and they
do not have to sink for ore. They drive straight
into the mountain, and the metal travels with its own
weight to the truck. I strenuously evade all hospitable
efforts to drag me up to it. Gold, silver, copper,
lead, antimony, mercury, coal, zinc, iron are all found
in British Columbia—a noble array. Mining has
been dull of recent years owing to long litigation.
Last June the Dominion Government re-enacted the
Lead Bounties Act, practically making lead worth
£18 sterling per long ton. There were good reasons
for it, as the United States impose enormous import
duty on the ore, also the cost of production is great,
and the freight rate to the London market on pig-
lead amounts to £4 per ton. At the coast Vancouver
Island has huge deposits of iron, copper, gold and
silver. All this and more of mining passes to and
fro in talk, generally of an evening—the days are
devoured of work and sport; a young man with a
head of distraught hair and melancholy eyes tells me
most of it—he is a miner. I wonder as I listen if his
hair would lie down flat with surprise if he found a
real enormous gold nugget one day in his life, and
if his miserable face could ever look pleased. Soon

I say good-bye to him, to Big Jim and his little
pretty wife, to Otto, to the explorer-woman who goes
not as the crow flies, but as the trail winds, to the
little wooden house among the eternal mountains—
to the spluttering log fire, to the happy hunters.

On the train I lean as usual from the car and smell
again the smell of Canada—pine and cedar, pine
and cedar—here is the muddy Fraser River laced
with emerald mountain streams; down the sides of
the cañon grows the burning bush, there are splashes
like blood on the rock-face of maple deeply red.
Here is a gold dredge at work on the river, here is
Agassiz, with her deserted orchards, where Mr.
Prain shot a bear. We run into a litter of pigs and
leave a steaming, throbbing corpse behind; here is
a little settlement called Cheam—I wonder what
homesick Surrey man named it so. At Harrison
Mills is a pond of water-lilies gleaming silver tones
in green sward, all girdled with mountains. Here the
turgid Fraser turns green, she is cleansed by some
miracle of the mud of her earlier courses; here is
a butterfly, here bracken, dandelion, clover, yarrow,
a hedged lane—this country is like England, like
England!

From the livid grasses of the prairie to the sunny
orchards, the bracken, the ivy, the pleasant, low-

pitched voices, from a desert of grass, of wheat, of
scrub, where the wolf-willow glimmers on the wind-
bitten wold, from the prairies to this paradise is
change indeed. Here in this other more beautiful
England, British Columbia, the roads wind in mossy
dells unsoiled of weary feet tramping to win a daily
pittance, unstained of the filth of cities, untamed,
unbroken; the bracken stands twenty feet high, the
cedar and arbutus grow down to the edge of the sea,
the deer and salmon share wood and water. I tread
its ways bemused with wonder, morose with the
impact of sensation. I suffer the strange faces
about me almost as a bodily hurt, for they are used
to this wonderful country, and look with the aloofness of incomprehension at my amaze. From Vancouver I take steamer to Victoria, the capital city of
British Columbia, and the great mart of Vancouver
Island, on which it is built. We steam for five or
six hours through the Straits of Georgia, threading
among the green islands with Mount Baker looking like Fujiyama, white-capped against an amethyst
sky; the gulls sway against the breeze, the under
wing dyed with pink reflected from the brilliant
sunset water. I wander curiously about the streets
of Victoria; they are wide and beautiful, just tilted
from the level of a sheer copy of the Old Country

by the Oriental bias. Here are the little yellow Japs and Chinks, with their quiet, busy ways, their ceaseless industrious coming and going. Their shops are here, their names line the streets, they are as much part of the social machine as are these high-nosed, slim, tall men and women who speak "army" from every pore and who *are* Victoria. The gardens are fenced from public view by clipped holly hedges, ivy grows joyously, a welcome sight never seen on the prairies. Here is a garden full of roses, Mrs. John Laing nodding on her long stalk; La France, the rascal who pays so ill for cutting and is so beautiful that one always finds garden-room for her in spite of her withery habits; Frau Karl Druschki, long, white, graceful; Dorothy Perkins, vigorous of growth; a brilliant dragon-fly poises over her—he looks a little weak in the wing, perhaps, but this is mid-October—he lingers round as though he remembers the pink clusters which must have made that rambler a glory when it was in full bloom; he is annoyed with "Dorothy," and goes over to Mrs. John Laing for comfort. This brilliant sea and sky, this island of flowers and sweet scents makes me envy the high-nosed ones who come to live here in the afternoon of life. At Oyster Cove, in Esquimault Harbour, Captain Williams walks in his big wading-boots among the apple-trees and wax-berries telling me all the dowdy things that can happen to oysters if they are not nicely managed. Wo Lung, whose long pigtail is wound round his head like a cap, goes down to the cove to grapple some up for me to taste; the Captain takes me down to the sea and shows how they are "planted" with sea-paths so that between he can walk round and turn them over whenever he wants to. It is like a sea garden, and its summer-house is a wooden hut on the raft where he sorts his oysters over. Wo Lung staggers away with a heavy load, and I follow the Captain up to the apple-orchard once more, wondering how many I am expected to "taste."

Inland, happy as man must have been when he first saw Eden, I wander between splendid avenues of balmy cedar that make a luxury of breathing; maple burns in crimson and gold against the deep rich green of the pines—brown and gold and green—green and gold and brown—it is like looking at Dante Rossetti's palette. One Martin Vannier drives me to Cowichan Bay, the landscape is pure joy every inch of the way. The roads are wide and well kept, edged with picturesque snake-fences almost hidden under brown-gold bracken; here is a rich orchard where the apples hang among their

leaves like little crimson Chinese lanterns, when the
sun strikes them the untouched bloom glows like
mauve violet. Here is a herd of red polls, fat and
contented in pasture that looks like parkland, mag-
nificently timbered. The blue jays chatter as we
pass, Mount Tzouhalem rises beside us, a burning
mountain in its radiant garb of autumn foliage. A
funny mongrel with a fox-terrier head, a setter body
and a Pomeranian tail attaches himself to our "rig"
and barks at every elderberry bush—somebody
must have given him some to eat at one time. On
the slope of a hill by Cowichan Bay is a pretty house
of wood that reveals itself as Buena Vista Hotel—
set in trees that would grace the noblest English
park. We unhitch Jimmy, the dapple grey who has
shied industriously at every blade of grass on the
road, and reward him with a feed of oats. The mongrel rejects my overtures, coupled though they are
with enticing smells of lunch, and makes for the bush
to hunt for elderberry-trees; he gives a friendly leer
from a clump of ferns and disappears for the afternoon. Men come and go—for lunch, for a drink, for
a word with our host, and I watch them enviously—
they all have guns, they all have setters, they all
roam these glorious woods from day to day; I am a
momentary sojourner who would so gladly stay for

ever, and I wonder that they can wear a mask of calmness whose heritage is set in these pleasant paths.

Martin discovers that it is little use going after pheasants, as we had intended, without a dog; so we borrow a line and spoon from our host, and go down on the bay to troll for salmon. The glittering bait whirls busily in our wake; we row up and down and round and about. The sun settles closelier among the mountains, the little breeze fades to a whimpering calm, the gulls scream greedily over their fishing, carrion crows flap heavy wings over the dead fish on the shore. The wet line is twisted round my hand lest a sudden jerk betrays my absent-mindedness to Martin—and in such a peace as is beyond praise, beyond description, the day wears toward sunset.

The whole atmosphere of this lovely island is opposite to that strenuous, bracing prairie-life I have recently passed through. There the days tingle with work, with the massing of moneys, the stress of toil. Here the climate is warm and sensuous, the most part of the settlers have small incomes and are content with the happiness of "enough" rather than the excitement of "more." I sit brooding on the comfortable lives gentlepeople live here in Nature's lovely garden island on incomes which in the old country mean penury with all its attendant humiliations and demoralizations; I am so engrossed with thought and bitter with envy for the people who own the beautiful acres on either hand that I forget the tiny thrill of the whirling spoon, and am nearly jerked out of the boat when a furious salmon finds himself hooked. I collect my scattered thoughts and begin to haul him in amid excited advice from Martin, but I am not quick enough. The line slacks for one instant, a great bar of indignant silver flashes into the air and deluges me with water, he has twisted himself free, and I am in horrible disgrace. Martin says he was a fifteen-pounder, and looks at me with such grief and scorn that I forget Vancouver Island and remember that I am out to fish. You see he was lost through clumsy playing, and Martin would forgive clumsy gaffing sooner than that. After long patience I get a three-pound rock-cod, and suffer the forbearance of my guide all the way back. I point out the beauty of the catch as his ruddy translucence fades to pallor streaked with brilliant yellow, and flushes again to red-brown, but the fifteen pounds of silver salmon hang in Martin's mind and I am not acquitted. I suggest that the lost magnificence may have been a "cohoe," but even that slight comfort is denied me—Martin says he was a fifteen-pound "spring," and I marvel at his quickness of sight.

A tired, bloody-jowled mongrel meets us with a yap of joy under the cedars and arbutus; I sneak past him with the rock-cod spiked on a stick (the horny fins are supposed to be poisonous); I do not even pat the dog as we pass, I suspect him from his torpidity and gore of being a much better sportsman than I have proved myself to be.

I find my ship of the night, the lady gardener of the Rockies, is not to "pass" after all; we meet again, and one drenching morn at four of the clock she and I, with her uncle and aunt, may be seen rowing dismally towards one of the little islands that cluster round Vancouver Island, where they have bought a large estate. This is the beginning of the rainy season. Her uncle gives me "tips" for the good of other Englishmen who are coming out.

"Tell 'em not to bring out silly spiral gaiters that let in the wet, but puttees for choice, or gaiters to button up the side and come well over the boot. Tell 'em to bring a gabardine, and learn how to shoe a horse, and how to do a little cobbling, and how to use saw, chisel, axe and plane."

I listen respectfully while I struggle to row in the bow; the oar is all right but the rowlock is broken, and I keep getting into disgrace because I can't keep time with stroke; also my hair is hanging in front of my face dripping like the eaves of a thatched roof, and it is difficult to see when the back in front of me bends. Presently "the boys" spy us from afar and bring the launch to the rescue.

What a beautiful place they have! I cannot wonder army people come out here, I only wonder any one keeps away. I am taken over the bay to troll with rod and line in the Siwash way. Four fathoms from spoon to lead, and two fathoms from lead to point of rod. We use cuttyhunk and a lead of about three ounces. I land some nice fish, and am only sorry that Martin is not here to see. His scornful eyes are a humiliating memory. My gardener friend is not only versed in horticulture; in a little dairy under giant Douglas firs I watch her churn the pale cream, and I stand gazing in ignorance, but faith, at the glass disc which is to "get clear when the butter comes." Fascinated I hover over the pile of golden grains washed and rewashed and washed again; her clever hands finally pat and mould it to the guise in which one is accustomed to meet butter. I watch her melt yeast cake, and help her stir the dough till our arms ache, the pleasant acrid yeasty smell fills the kitchen. We troll the bay for more

fish, and catch a big "cohoe" who gives us great
sport and a cod who gives us an excellent breakfast;
we tramp the woods with a ·25/20 Winchester and
stock the larder with venison because "the deer have
eaten up all Auntie's winter cabbage."

In the sunset we walk, we two moderns, in the
primal glades discussing the Fabian Society,
eugenics, Brieux, Ibsen, Tolstoy, all the questions
and question-makers that have been born of our
teeming population and the stress of civilization.

"Incongruous in such a setting," I say at last, but
she does not agree.

"Here is the young world to be built. Where
else should be discussed the lesson of the old?" she
says.

"What has it taught us?" I ask, being older and
less buoyant.

"That all's well with the world! That races, like
the flame, go upward! That the new is better than
the old, that the future is greater than tradition."

British Columbia is opening up every year; the
Grand Trunk Pacific will soon make the Kitsumga-
lum Valley a rival in fruit-growing with the Okanagan. The province is thickly grown with valuable
trees, it has the sea, it has minerals, it is rich beyond
belief in every natural beauty. It is a sportsman's

paradise where range the bear—black, grizzly, cinnamon; the moose, caribou, deer, wapiti or elk, the bighorn, or Rocky Mountain sheep, of all Canadian game the most wary and difficult to bag (every head brought down represents honest hard work and straight shooting); the mountain goat abounds, that singular bearded beast, most daring of all mountain climbers; wolves; puma, or cougar, often called panther or mountain lion; lynx; antelope; besides the small game: foxes, hares, rabbits, mink, fisher martin, sable, otter, beaver, muskrat, wolverine and the rest. Although few persons, however keen, would visit this province merely for the sake of its wing shooting, yet it is undeniable that, with the exception of Manitoba, Alberta, Saskatchewan and Athabasca, a man may find as much work for his breechloader here as anywhere abroad. Five species of grouse, and vast quantities of wildfowl, from swans to teal, abound in suitable localities. The marshes of the Columbia swarm with mallard and other choice duck in the autumn; the Arrow Lakes and the upper valley of the Fraser form a trough much frequented by the wild geese during their migrations, and the fiords and sounds of the coast shelter great flocks of wildfowl throughout the winter —the winters of the Pacific are very much less rigorous than those of the Atlantic, and a very large proportion of the birds do not go farther south than Vancouver Island.

The fishing is so remarkable that no one can realize the quantities of salmon and trout to be found in the streams till he or she has visited British Columbia.

The province is divided into eight districts, each of which would require a whole book to set forth its peculiarities of soil, climate, mineral and timber resources and diversity of scenery! There is the Kootenay district, drained by the Columbia and Kootenay rivers, which combines in odd juxtaposition fruit orchards and copper mines. There is Yale, the garden of British Columbia, with its lakes and sunny orchards; Lillooet, the pastoral country devoted to dairying and cattle raising; there is Westminster, which includes the fertile valley of the Lower Fraser, famous for its lumbering and salmon canning industries—unfortunately the canneries are closed at this time of the year and I do not see over them; Cariboo and Cassiar, great unexploited tracts of close on 200,000,000 acres which look to the new Grand Trunk Pacific Railway to bring settlers to mine for gold and work the fertile belts; there are the Comox district and Vancouver Island, where fruits are prolific and fishing, quartz mining, copper smelting, whaling and shipbuilding are staple industries.

Victoria, the capital of British Columbia, is an important business and industrial centre. It shares with Vancouver the northern trade and that of the interior; the vessels entered and cleared during 1906–7 were 3,625, and of these 2,077 were foreign. It is the first port of call for the trans-Pacific liners and northern steamers, as well as all the big freighters which round the Horn for Puget Sound points.

Labour is scarce and dear. Women can command in domestic service anything from fifteen to thirty-five dollars a month with board.

In brilliant sunshine I leave Vancouver, gathered like a child to the breast of the mountains, and turn my face to the east again. On the prairie tract the train gets snowed up at Maple Creek; after the tropical vegetation, the rugged magnificence of British Columbia, these lowly hills and vast treeless spaces covered with snow under a blue-green sky are odd indeed. We wait on the train day after day, discussing the country's platitude, topographical and domestic, watching the gophers playing on the glittering snow by the track. This is an unusually early blizzard, and people tell storm stories in the intervals

of snowball fights, and questioning the worried conductor about the progress of the two snow-ploughs in front which are endeavouring to clear the way.

I am on the "home trail." Soon this brilliant air, this boundless country will be out of touch and sight, will have given place to the misty greys of tiny populous England.

CHAPTER IX

THE train pulls away from Winnipeg, the nigger porter assiduously portions me my pet berth, "No. 2 Lower," the dining-car conductor bustles about distilling odours of bacon and coffee every time he opens the door of his car. . . . I am on the eastward train and my face is set towards home.

Let no one think he can come to the young North-West and leave it with joy. Lightly enough I came three months ago, lightly enough I took the trail towards the sunset, lightly enough I trod the magic land that leaves its mark for ever on the heart. The process is so unconscious. I never knew as I trod the prairie grasses and caught the perfume of the low roses brushing by my skirt, I never knew as I looked towards the mountains in the sunset that these once tasted leave an everlasting hunger for more; there was no way of knowing that when I followed the lean trail it would never cease to beckon, only now as I turn eastward do I learn the thing that has happened. Another song to haunt the silences till death.

There is the song of remembered childhood—we all hear it at times—by "moonlight or by candle-light"; there is the song of the first kiss of first love; there is the song of the beloved waxen dead we laid to earth with bitter grief; there is the song of the secret hours when none but ourselves know how the soul lost or won, how good or how bad the record was made—every one of us has that song to haunt the heart; but not all of us has added to the list with this song of the West that is started for me, and which I have neither power to still nor will to resent. It is a song of labour, hardship, loneliness, of great rewards, of unfettered life, of limitless oppor-tunities. A song of hope, of freedom; a song of a happy land.

I suppose it is the savage in us that responds to the wild waste places, the savage which looks with eyes of sympathy on the face of Nature when we find her virgin, naked, unashamed. I don't know—one doesn't analyze these emotions if one is wise. But I do know that the beaten roads and easy paths of England seem tame and tiresome to feet that have followed the trail through bush and scrub, by creek and slough, under a boundless sky with the sun for sign-post and the warm, wild wind for friend. It is hopeless to urban ears to talk of the exhilaration that clutches at the heart when one finds oneself stripped of the "conveniences" of life—the intolerable hideous yoke of comforts that civilization binds on our backs from birth who live in settled lands. The uplifting of the heart when it finds itself free and face to face with primal conditions is not to be told in words to such as have not tasted. But it waits in Canada in great draughts for those who have the courage to seek it, wine for the brave heart. There is no call in her for those who are tainted with the poisonous love of cities; in the name of mercy let such stay in Europe. Dreaming hearts that love the mourn of a deep-throated wind in trees, that feel the pulse of a secret never solved in the touch of loam and leaf-mould, the beginning and the end of philosophies and fears in the sowing and the reaping, who keep a steadfast face to fate, not from ignorance but knowledge, who offer a beautiful service to Nature—those are the souls to win the wild, to garner happiness in every twist of the seasons, to bide the rewards of labour in unmurmuring patience.

As I look regretfully at the landscape slipping from me with every throb of the train, hoarding jealous memories of every acre as it passes, I remember a great deal that Mr. Larcombe in Manitoba said about the pity of people coming out and buying land cheap for speculative purposes, the unfairness of it to the workers. He advocated buying land with a view to settling it, and was ardently anxious that English capitalists should settle vast tracts with English settlers. I hear his mellow old voice droning out a scheme as we drive about his prosperous acres.

"Why will not an English capitalist purchase several thousand acres of land with a view to settling British farmers on it. The land could be divided into farms as at present, namely, 160 acres, and let at a rental of ten per cent. of the purchase money, allowing the tenants option of purchase at any time within ten years by giving the original purchaser fifty per cent. on the purchase. Say the capitalist buys at ten dollars an acre and re-sells at fifteen, giving the tenant option of purchase at any time in ten years, drawing till such time ten per cent. interest on the original outlay; it should be possible to adjust the percentage and purchase money to give the settler stock and farm implements as well as land. There seems no reason why 20,000 settlers could not be arranged for in this way with profit to both first purchaser and the man who settles; the latter will avoid the handicap of distance which tells so heavily on the settlers on free homesteads. The best-placed land is already sold. It is dearer now-a-days to get land at a gift than to buy it where there are opportunities."

I think that was the scheme he outlined, it was a warm sleepy day and I was being lulled into slumber by the dolorous chant of his voice, when he became highly excited over the tariff question and I had to wake up and appear to know what he was talking about.

"Why don't English manufacturers come here and build plant near Winnipeg for making farm implements?" he asked fiercely. "The Americans are fetching raw materials from the Kootenays at twenty per cent. duty, then making the stuff in America and bringing it over here at another duty of thirty per cent., thus making a duty of fifty per cent. on the farm implements bought in Canada. The preferential tariff is no good, it is only a two cent preference. All English goods should be allowed in free, the ocean rate is so small that that would make a great difference to our trade. As things are we are building up American millionaires out of the hard earnings of our Western farmers.

There should be no tariff on any English goods, Canada should be as free to England as England to us. Then she would get her revenues from direct taxation, which she could well afford, seeing she would be getting her goods so much cheaper. Probably twenty or thirty per cent. of moneys collected under tariff revenue is paid to excise officers whose duty it is to watch Canada's shores."

He looked at my automatic smile of acquiescence and suddenly accused me of utter tariffic ignorance. I admitted it, I remember, and was thereupon bitterly accused of being behind the times, also of being a perfidious deceiver.

"Why, I saw in the paper that you were speaking to the presswomen of Winnipeg on female suffrage."

I hastened to explain and left him only half enlightened, I fear; he did not tell me any more schemes, but he told me a great deal about farming and was infinitely kind, the nice old man. I hope he ended by forgiving my political ignorance.

As a matter of fact I had said a few words to the presswomen of Winnipeg when they very courteously entertained me to a luncheon, and I had spoken on the suffrage because I saw it was a topic that both interested and shocked. I only asked them to reserve judgment on the question till they had been over to England and studied the working conditions for women at first hand. And I was wrongly reported, too, I remember. One paper said I had said that Mrs. Humphry Ward had never done a day's work in her life! Mrs. Humphry Ward! who has given us the *History of David Grieve*, and *Robert Elsmere*, and *William Ashe*, and *Marcella*! What I really said was that probably she had never had to work day in and day out for her very life. My farmer friend was quite right in being shocked at my ignorance of politics. I know so little of them that I think only the units of the community, irrespective of rank and sex and age, who can pass a standard examination on present politics and political history should have a vote. Only those. We might select from among us in that way brains fitted to choose the governing brains.

So musing, remembering, watching the country slip by, we clang at last into Ottawa, the capital of Canada, at an untoward hour on a frosty morn, where Meg and Gaston greet me shivering and smiling.

One thing which has struck me very forcibly about the people of the country is their "insularity," their narrowed horizon. Frequently in passing from province to province I have been impelled by admiration to say, "What a beautiful country this is," meaning always Canada as compared with what I know of the rest of the world. And always my hearer has taken me to mean, not Canada, not even his own province, not even that, but just his own town or hamlet. Time after time I was met by this limited outlook, time after time I hit up against this barrier and found that to expect imperial thought or argument was like fighting with a pudding.

"What do you think of this country?" has been a question asked me more than any other, and it took me a very long time to realize that I must answer not for the Dominion, but for the few square miles around me; with the attrition of other minds and the facilities for travel which added railways will offer that narrow view will doubtless widen; and anyway it argues some pride of locality, some interest in comparisons of attribute and progress, however small. Prides are good for the individual, for the municipality, for the race, they carry virtues of strength and independence in their train, and no one will deny that the Canadian is proud, even to boastfulness, of his land, its size, its progress, its possibilities, so proud that he errs at times on the side of believing no other prides in the world should have hearing but his own. There are the faults and virtues of a young people to be noticed on every hand, and I—sated with the civilization of London —understand and envy the fierce youth and un- tamed ambition which beat in the heart of this land. All its future is before it; if it has not a background of glorious history it has the making of it in hand with all the histories of the world to guide it to glory.

There is no Established Church in Canada. There is none of the struggle or the ennobling of religious dissent; every congregation, Roman Catholic, Church of England, Presbyterian and the rest supports its own pastors. And it suffers from no lack of them or of churches. In fact, I am struck with what appeals to me as a plethora of religious edifices on every hand. Toronto has 218 churches! In some parts of the prairie, notably in Saskatchewan, I found a demand for young Church of England men, to help with the training of the catechists, ordained men to drive from point to point of the diocese and perform the duties neces- sarily left undone by the men in training. Arch- deacon Lloyd of Prince Albert, Saskatchewan, is the superintendent of catechists, and would, I imagine, answer readily all inquiries on the subject. I know the haughty cleric in the Old Country, and

am envious to see how the familiar estate will look
in the New, stripped of the prestige which its position gives it in England. It seems to me that what
it loses in snobbery it gains in vital energy.
Whether the aim be a worthy one or no the young
men of the Church know that their incomes depend
on the way they please and handle their congrega-
tions. It behoves a clergyman to work hard in
Canada, like every one else; he can never slacken
on the tenure of a fat living, he must be up and
doing or his income will abate, his popularity de-
cline, and finally his flock fail to support him. I
have thought a great deal about the two methods,
the Established and Disestablished, and I must
admit that our Old Country way appeals to me as
more dignified and more likely to aid honesty than
the Canadian way. Not energy, perhaps, but independence, and with independence commonly goes
honesty. I would sooner fight the haughtiest pride
in my Rector than feel he depended on his manner
to me and mine for his daily bread. This is rather
in the way of rumination than statement. I have
not studied either condition closely enough to
venture to have a decided opinion. I had a long
talk with a young Irish curate in Manitoba one day:
he said his people were good to him, his labour

interested him, he loved the climate, and his horse was his greatest friend. All he wanted was a wife, and he was coming overseas to find one in his next holiday. He told me he would not go back for any-thing, not for all the bouts of homesickness he some-times had to fight. This with a twinkling Celtic eye, and a beautiful brogue that would lure any wandering sheep back to the fold. I found after-wards that he was a very popular young man, and therefore was well supported by his flock.

The Presbyterian and other sects have as large followings as the Church of England; I am, indeed, not sure that the latter does not come rather far down in the statistical table.

If the Dominion Government does not support its churches it does most liberally and wisely aid its hospitals. If a choice between the two causes had to be made in every land I would most warmly back the choice of Canada. Look after the bodies, help the hospitals, give them prestige and status: let none be ashamed to use them. With healthy, happy bodies the people is liable to have happy, healthy souls. I can see a maelstrom of argument whirling round that statement—I know many an eminent divine who would fight it tooth and nail; but I believe it is true.

EASTWARD BOUND

The whole of Canada is terraced with Governments; there is the great Dominion Government, which sits at Ottawa and controls the affairs of the nation as a whole. Under it are the Provincial Governments, each working with its own Premier, its own parliament, its own social system. The Provincial Governments are by no means to be lightly considered as we consider the word provincial over in England. A "province" means a country as large as France or Germany, and its Premier has great powers. The provinces are divided up into municipalities and so on, and ranging among these divisions and subdivisions of power are strange errant forces of enormous wealth and influence, governments within governments reigning, controlling, directing, making men, making money; great companies with chartered rights and immense land-holdings—the Hudson Bay Company and the Canadian Pacific Railway Company. There are other railroads coming along, the Canadian Northern has been running some time, and the Grand Trunk Pacific nears completion among others, but in the West the Canadian Pacific Railway towers by reason of its priority, and no other fur company can touch the Hudson Bay for that same reason. Considering the complexity of the

219

machinery it seems extraordinary that Canada governs herself as peacefully and as smoothly as she does. I am travelling near General Election time, and find tales of "graft" and corruption on every hand, tales which steady men smile at, and which apparently have no influence on the confidence which Canada feels in her existing government, seeing she re-elects it wholeheartedly.

I am impressed by the wonderful number of Scotchmen who succeed in the New Land. He is welcomed straight off as a likely success and the Englishman is instantly expected to be a failure. They must have earned these reputations. The Galicians are a handsome race of a much lower type than the Scotch, and prove very adaptable settlers, with a great ambition to own stock. The Jews are only found in cities, they are commercial parasites and no good on the land. There is hardly one successful Jew farmer in Canada. Seeing that they came originally of a pastoral race the fact is singular and interesting; we in England—a nation of commerce—have given them so much room that our country has become a sort of secondary Palestine! Some derelict Jews totally unsuited to Canadian conditions arrived at one of the centres for immigrants and were refused admission to the country. Application was made to the Hirsch Fund officials to deport them, and it was promised they should be sent "home." So they were. To Liverpool.

Many of the tragedies of failure in emigration revolve round the ignorance of the prospective settler of what qualifications are necessary to make prosperity in Canada likely. The woman who applied for a post as a teacher in a Methodist Ladies' College and could only produce a certificate for dancing in support of her application was not unusually silly. Another "skilled workman" who wanted to settle in Canada was asked what his trade was. He said he was a doll's-eye maker. It is these unintelligent venturers who are the drug-bats of the Empire. I like that word drug-bats. I was walking down a country road in England one day when I saw on a little notice-board by the roadside a warning about the "improper use of drug-bats," and became deeply exercised in mind as to what this strange beast was. I thought of Dracula, of vampire bats, of strange, silent, flitting shapes that might haunt the brows through open bedroom windows at night and inflict deadly opiate bites on slumbering innocents. They were all wide of the truth. I learned in time that a drug-bat is a skid-pan, in other words a primitive brake which not only reduces speed, but also cuts up a well-made road. I suppose the word was originally "drag-back," but see how the soft blurred Surrey voices have made of it a picturesque, romantic, wonderful thing! But the stern significance of it remains unsoftened, it is still a skid-pan, a harmful brake, and that is what every hasty, unsuitable emigrant, rich or poor, noble or humble, is on the progress of the Empire.

CHAPTER X

THE ART OF CANADA

" DOES Art make for decadence? " The question calls to mind many a warm, wordy warfare in London's debating societies, when the battle invariably ended with a struggle in definitions. What is Art? What is decadence? And never did two agree, and never have I heard the initial question definitely settled. The historian would always rise with his mouldy tales of Greece and Rome and the artistic craftsman would for ever retort with his question, " Would you stay civilization then, for civilization always brings the cult of beauty in its train? "

I had a whiff of it on the Rocky Mountains when a sunburnt Canadian flung at me that he was " Real glad this country had no Art, it meant the beginning of the end in every sane man's mind."

But his flattered grin when I replied that in that case Canada was on the point of instant dissolution, for it made the finest enamel of any I had ever seen, Battersea and Limoges not excepted, suggested to me that his view was based on jealousy rather than study. I am inclined to believe that a great number of the crude prides in crudity that I collected from Canadians in the notes of my sojourn had their birth in a similar emotion. There is growing, however, a feeling for Art. Painting and literature are yet to come; the kindest critic could hardly say that either has yet achieved expression at a master's hand; but here and there is an apostle of beauty. In a land of such exceeding natural loveliness it would be strange if this were not so, even in these early days of settlement and struggle.

The enamel I had known and admired long before I traced it to its source. Of a very fine surface and brilliant in colour I had chosen stray pieces to bring back to England, during my first visit, always deploring, when I saw my samples, the difficulty of getting a good design. On a hot day in Montreal I found the heart of the industry, and Mr. Hemming took me over the factory, where I laid bare to him the disturbance I always suffered in seeing the frequently ugly and sometimes vulgar designs to which the beautiful medium was set. So far as I may be permitted to judge, it seemed to me that his artists' desire was always to show a range of colour in their designs, rather than doing what they might well have done, restricting colour and form to the very simplest and letting the exquisite enamel speak for itself. When we passed from this carping talk to look at processes I was free to admire the patience and care that have gone to make Canadian enamel what it is. To my unlearned mind the joy and pride the manager takes in his pet water-supply in the tank for cooling dyes was a trifle obscure, but obviously the dirty water had some grave virtue, counted of great moment and concern. I learned with interest that the staff know to a hair's-breadth the thickness of the ground metal and the amount of enamel that the raised pattern will hold, so by a finely poised balance of thicknesses they equalize the dangerous differences of time that silver and enamel take to cool. They spoke with scorn of the English method of preventing unequal cooling and consequent splitting, which is to enamel *both* sides of the object in hand. It is a good way for amateurs, they told me, easy and extravagant. They showed me also with the same scorn a sample of "English finish." I recognized at once the class of ware which we tolerate over here, coarse and pimply in texture; putting beside it a piece of the Montreal work, I was again amazed at the fineness of surface, the limpid depth of finely polished colour in the latter.

They had another ware at this factory which was interesting, "silver deposit" they called it, a clumsy

name for a beautiful thing. By some secret process
they superimpose sterling silver or pure gold on to
glass and china, welding both in indissoluble union.
I admired the ware most sincerely, but again made a
protest about the designs; some were beautiful,
simple, suave, but a number had an unfortunate
leaning to the angularities and meaningless vagaries
of "L'Art nouveau." When I protested about the
ugly shape of a china teapot which had been en-
riched by the silver deposit I found English manufacturers in disgrace. They will not send out what
is asked for, only what they think ought to be
wanted; one can hardly conceive a more aggravating
method in business. I made a mental note to take
any opportunity that might present itself on my return to the old country to tell English manufacturers what was said of them in Montreal. The old
method of slipping a framework of design in silver
or gold on to glass or china is incomparably bettered
by this method of the Hemming factory; in the old
way the metal was a refuge for dust and dirt, besides
being liable to bending and loosening. By the new
process glass and metal are one with obvious advantages. I left the factory filled with a vicarious joy in
work; there is great pleasure in seeing men working
arduously at labours which they love.

I was fated to come in contact on the same day with much that Canada boasts of applied art; for a note waited at the hotel when I got in from the enamel factory asking me to come and see some French-Canadian fabrics. I was ready packed, had an hour to spare, and went. How the air smelt of cedar! When I was little we used to have cedar-wood pencils at school, and I remember sitting sniffing the faint perfume (which always grew more elusive as the pencil got greasier) while my unwilling mind followed the intricacies of "x" on the blackboard. I have forgotten the vagaries of "x," but I vividly recall the sweet smell of cedar, and there it was in the nostrils then, full-bodied and fresh, a real grown-up cedar smell mixed with pines, and sometimes an indescribable heavy, luscious sensuous smell from a fruit orchard on Mount Royal. I was welcomed with tea and shown the French-Canadian hand-woven linen curtains made of home-spun flax and darned with good patterns in coloured wools. They were of a coarsish texture, with a fine silky gloss in the thread; hand-woven blankets, too, made of home-spun wool, light and warm and very pleasing. No crudeness in that work. There spoke the dignity of tradition, the legended lore of an established race, and the staid quality of long experience. I was warm with appreciation when suddenly a ruddy-faced man of Belial foisted the old quarrel of England *v.* Canada upon me once more. He had a horrific yarn to tell of an eminent English Colonial official (named) who asked what the capital of Canada was. I said that doubtless he would learn in due course when Canada had settled it for herself; a retort that infuriated him to the last degree as he was from Ottawa, and there were people from Toronto present as well as the Montrealers. The fight waxed and waned and waxed again till I rushed for my train carrying with me mixed memories. Whenever I remember home-spun fabrics warm and fleecy, I must see peering over them a red face pregnant with quarrel. Those curtains and blankets, though out of Canada, are hardly of it. They belong to the civilization from which came Grand Pré, Evangeline and the rest; they are not evolved, like the enamel is, from the composite people which calls itself Canadian, any more than the bead-work woven and the supple skins of caribou tanned by the Indians can be called Canadian.

A chapter on Art would be sadly shorn of truth did I omit to mention a certain apostle of interior decoration, and her work. At distant points of the long travel from Quebec to Victoria I found hotels

which received me with subdued, consistent colour
schemes, with broad effects of decoration, and unexpected knowledge in choice furniture, of brasses, of
pictures. The first I saw was at Quebec; high over
the brilliant St. Lawrence hung the spires of the
Château Frontenac, and in it were vistas of green
tapestries and carpets made beautiful with fine old
Dutch brass. Spoilt by Europe and still unused to
the rawness of a young country, I remember taking
the pleasant place rather for granted, and giving it
only the tribute of an approving glance; by the
time I reached Montreal, however, I had learned
other, and was thankful when I found the Place
Viger also individual and restful in colour and design. Later, as I neared Winnipeg, I had arrived at
the stage of hoping that the Alexandra Hotel might
evidence this unusual taste; when I went into it,
travel-stained and unutterably weary, it was good
to be welcomed again by the comfort of chosen
colours and fabrics. It is not easy to describe the
gratitude with which I sat to write in the gold and
brown drawing-room, rested in every nerve by the
courage and the calm of its scheme of decoration. I
began to suspect some master eye in the employ of
the Canadian Pacific Railway, seeing it was always
Canadian Pacific Railway hotels which were so nice,

and to bow in my mind to the discretion of the Director in choosing him. Such was the character of the arrangement of these hotels that they have become starred in my memory of travel as very points of rest, as oases in that desert of interminable motion and dust. I remember them all;—the hunting frescoes in the lounge at Banff, the quaint Egyptian effects in the dining-hall at Vancouver, the fine conventional posters that line the corridors in the Empress at Victoria, and the daring ceiling in the dining-room there which hangs overhead heavy with carved mahogany and panels of green. By the time I reached Banff I had learned that the artist who designed for the Canadian Pacific Railway was Mrs. Hayter Reid, wife of the Director of Hotels! I had learned to understand the love of colour that must impel this woman, her keen sense of proportion, an attribute vital to success in art and impossible to instil where lacking. It was that sense which made Josiah Wedgwood the greatest master in English ceramics apart from his patient industry in chemical research and the discovery of the jasper ware that sealed his fame. I had grown to know in my own mind that the things which were not perfect, here and there, were due to some extraneous reason and were not her work at all. Thus sure could one grow of the sense of beauty and of fitness that permeated her work. At Vancouver we met. A woman handsome beyond the ordinary, vivid, picturesque, built mentally and physically on large lines, with an impulsive vitality in word, in glance and gesture. I found her a genuine Bohemian in the finest sense of the word; frank, sincere and original. In ten minutes from meeting I was in the thick of her work, watching her select papers and match paint among a troop of workmen who were to make a new smoking-room and were waiting her orders. She spoke in a flux of energy, scattering objections where they gathered; rousing them where a false peace reigned. A thousand problems found a thousand solutions instantly at her hands. She was like a dominant seventh, always herself on the pitch of ecstasy, always leaving her resolution of tonic calm behind. After an hour of tempestuous labour, "Come," she said, "I only have a few hours here, let us hunt for curios." And willy-nilly out I went, hatless, breathless with that whirlwind of a woman into the sunny Vancouver streets, plunging into stores and odd corners where Indian goods and Japanese goods and French-Canadian home-spuns were chosen and rejected in bewildering array. I must always remember that splendid creature, with the generous warmth radiating from her smiling eyes, framed, as I saw her then, in the wide streets of the lovely Pacific city, the mountains and the sea for background.

In connection with art and artists I am constrained to remember certain other sensitive and cultured souls which it was my fortune to meet in Canada, salt of the intellectual world, pioneers of thought, invaluable influences for the coming generation. There are others, but I can only write of those I met; one ardent collector and connoisseur whom I missed meeting, much to my regret, was Sir William Van Horn. Chief among the unforgettable was Dr. Herridge, the famous Presbyterian preacher, author of *The Orbit of Life* and *Coign of Vantage*. Before we met I heard a woman say of him, "He prefers a good phrase to a good dinner," a description which rang in my ears for many a day, for the tone of indulgent scorn in which it was said roused in me a totally different series of emotions to those intended by the speaker. I felt a sincere admiration for such a literary taste as was evidenced by such a criticism, and a burning compassion for the critic. When we met eventually I found a tall, austere man, swarthy, sardonic, with eyes of a stormy brilliance and a manner which suggested restlessness held rigidly to calm. I strayed into his church, learning for the first time in my life the limpid simplicity of a Presbyterian service, and discovered his sermons to be of an unusual order—brilliant, epigrammatic and as far removed from the ordinary chatter of the pulpit as an essay by G. B. Shaw from a *Child's Guide to Knowledge*. He jolted one from the rut of intellectual indolence by gibing at "indignant spasms of respectability" and deriding the "slothful half-truths of convention" till the startled brain, stung to attention from the average somnolence of sermon-time, was braced to receive the full shock of oratory.

A keen sense of humour dominates his method; in private life it breaks out into secular wit. I remember one bitter night sitting in the Rink with a large gathering to hear a choral concert. It was so cold that the music became tiresome, and at last I said testily—

"It's pathetic to hear scores of obvious spinsters singing over and over again, 'Unto us a son is given.'"

His harsh mouth twisted into a smile.

"Madam," he paraphrased, "that is the triumph of hope over inexperience."

I asked him once why he did not come to London and gather about him, as he inevitably would, an appreciative congregation of cultured Bohemians. The rebuke was simple : " Madam, I have a congregation here, why should I leave it ? " A strange man; for all the tempestuous unrest of his eyes a student, a scholar, patient !

Talking of unusual personalities reminds me of Miss Cora Hind; there is a woman ! Small, slight, quick of movement and speech, with pince-nez and workmanlike clothes. She is commercial editor of the biggest daily paper in the Western Dominion, the *Winnipeg Free Press;* many a hard tale she can tell of drives in the autumn weather from farm to farm when she has been out estimating the year's crop on behalf of her paper. Hard-headed and practical, and something of a sociological dreamer, she would rank with the best women thinkers over here, and in her own city is regarded with marvel not unmixed with fear. From Winnipeg to Calgary I found her recognized as an authority on stock breeding, a reputation that called for unstinted praise from every man who spoke of her, and made some women, to my infinite amusement, sniff. Yes, that is the word, Sniff. I found in her the side least widely known. We met in Winnipeg, where I was kept for a couple of days in my room at the hotel glued to the telephone waiting for

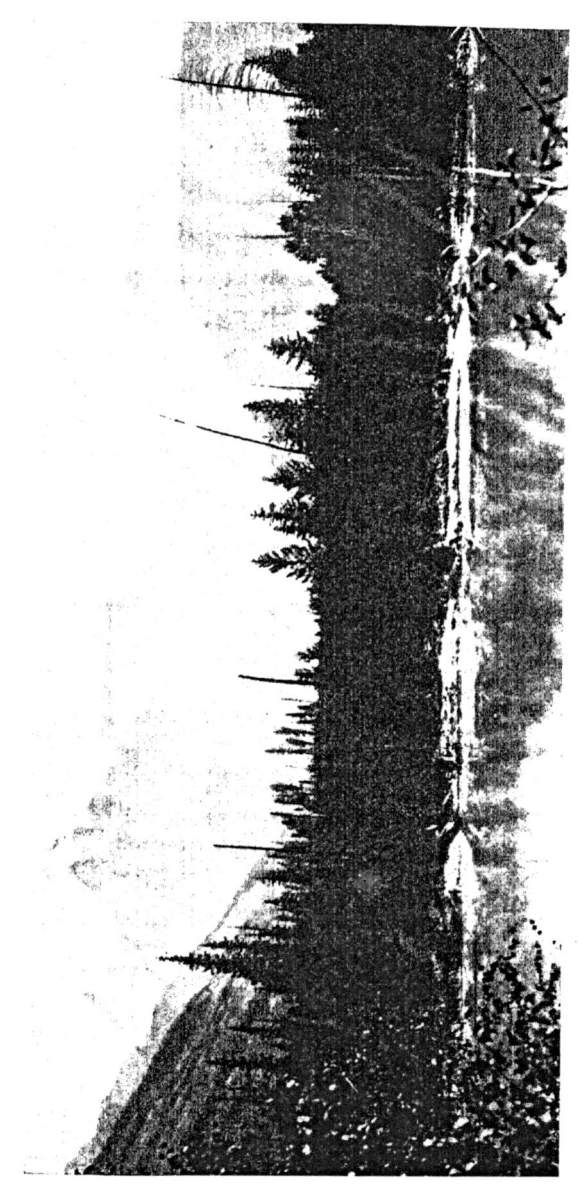

official orders; a programme of inaction which developed a devastating condition of home-sickness; I would sit at my table trying to write, my mind straying to the bracken and heather of England while I watched the sun beat hot on the flat prairie city, and fashion a ring of orange flame to wed her withal at sunset; I would scurry down to meals leaving a train of messages as to my whereabouts, and scurry back to wait for the bell that would not ring when this little woman heard of the sister journalist within her gates and carried me off to her flat, genial and gentle as a mother with a sick child. Goodness knows why, but she did the nicest thing in the world. She let me lay tea! Possibly it was the hint of home life . . . how kind she was! And from that moment my stay in Winnipeg was busy and happy throughout. We talked together, and I found in her, remote though she is from the movement, a student of eugenics. "There is much more interest taken in breeding hogs in Western Canada than there is in breeding children," she said, deploring the vice of ignorance which masks itself as modesty and leaves the stain of its incompetence on generation after generation. I asked her how she came to have adopted this bachelor way of life, to have acquired the freedom of thought and simplicity of outlook which made her indeed so charming, but was so removed from the Canadian ideal of what is best in woman. "I come of a protesting stock," she said, and I learned she had pioneer and Huguenot blood in her veins. She busied herself with introductions for the rest of my journey, so that I should not be lonely any more. One of her descriptions lingers in my memory—"You'll find him white all through and straight as a string!"

I suppose I lay myself open to controversy when I say I count Miss Hind an artist. She would not say so of herself. But it has always seemed to me that the man or woman who takes a delight in work and bends all the intelligence to doing it well, who stints nothing of time or labour to obtain the best results, is an artist whatever form the work takes. The statement opens a wide field for debate. I don't know how far it would work out.

Canada makes singers. As the harsh, bracing air of the Yorkshire wolds seems to string its children's throats to singing pitch, so does the brilliant climate over there. One woman with a voice of velvet and silver is "Maria Ricardi" (Miss Lily Gibbs at home).

I heard her voice first in a romantic setting—it was during my first visit to Canada during a journey from Ottawa to Toronto. We were flying through a darkness that might be felt, a heavy murk hung like a blanket over the world, we travelled in the discomfort of close stuffy heat, and many of us went to the platform at the end of the car gasping for breath. In the narrow space we talked with the easy fellowship of travellers, watching the darkness when it was stabbed with a jagged sword of light, listening to the roar of the thunder above the rattle of the train and welcoming the blessed rain when, at last, it teemed upon us. We jostled together undismayed by the wet, and watched the scene; now a flash would show the glitter of water below our wheels, we were crossing a bridge—now we would have a second's glimpse of rolling pastures as we passed a lonely homestead —now a bracken-clad ravine; and now we would have an instantaneous vision of tapering pines against the sky. It felt like being inside a great camera with some Titanic hand pressing the button here and there to impress snap-shot pictures upon the sensitive films of memory. We were an hour and three-quarters late (more than anything else except the Experimental Farms I found the lateness of the trains drove home to my consciousness the gigantic size of Canada). We were not dallying with time; the big black engine, so unlike the cosy little round ones of England, "had a hustle on," and we were all wearying for the lights of Toronto. I leaned out as far as I dared and looked into the night—in such wild hours the pulses stir and the brain reels with grim thoughts; it did not strike strangely when a voice broke into the darkness with the mad song from *Lucia di Lammermoor*. It was born of the storm—a dream-voice, a goblin-voice— I resented being told by my fellow-travellers in awe-stricken tones that Maria Ricardi was travelling with us, and that "It must hurt her throat, sure, to sing in the wind and rain."

I heard that beautiful voice last amid the perfume of the flowers, the glitter of jewels and lights in a London concert hall. Instantly it ravished me from civilization into darkness, I felt the sting of rain upon my face and saw again the lightning-born pictures of that night.

Another Canadian musician is Guy Maingy, an artist of great genius and extraordinary ill-luck.

So many other interesting and amusing people I met: Miss Hughes, the Provincial Librarian of Alberta, a quaint, demure, silent little person with a really remarkable power of observation and expression; Mrs. Bennett of Regina, with the beautiful eyes and motherly way, who succeeded so nicely in looking unconcerned when I smoked a cigarette one day

after a particularly hard wrestle with pen and ink.
I shall always remember that courteous calm, it
utterly deceived me, and I smoked in comfort.
Months afterwards in a London theatre I met Mr.
Hook of the Regina " daily " (I forget its name), and
he told me I had considerably damaged an otherwise
fair reputation by smoking. Which was very sad
and horrible for me, but very nice for the gossips. I
always believe gossip-mongers keep a warm place in
their hearts for people who shock them. They must.
Things would be so dull for them without shocks.

I remember, too, how well I remember, a lovely
face, a low voice, a cultured, beautiful mind with
which I communed for an hour at Victoria—Mrs.
Fitz Gibbon—the most fragrant personality I met in
my travels. She gave the idea of one who walked
unaware of earth with face to the stars.

An amusing person was the prairie follower. I
arrived at a little wooden prairie city one night and
proceeded as usual the first thing next morning to
the Board of Trade official with my introductions,
and a request to see something of the country round
about. I was received among two or three settlers
and farmers as usual, and found every resource of
officialdom again as usual laid with quick kindliness
at my feet. I remember saying I wanted to drive

out to a homestead and talk to a new settler's wife, if
there were such to be found within driving distance.
Such was to be found, I learned, and arrangements
would be made to take me there. "Was I staying at
the X——?" mentioning the only hotel. I was.
Exit, to wander round the wooden sidewalks, to buy
some stamps, to linger a little outside a rifle store
and listen to the strange crop-figures offered by a
local farmer to some one he wanted to impress;
Canadians are never correct in numbers. Their
replies are always tinged with a little of their hope—
and then back to the hotel to write. At the door a
rig and a young-old man. He asked me if I did
not wish to see So-and-So's farm. I said "Yes," and
without more ado mounted into the little seat beside
him between the spidery wheels, telling myself that
this Board of Trade official excelled all I had ever
met for quickness in attending to the wants of a
wandering journalist. We drove on and on, over
miles of prairie, bumping and joggling across the
rich black loam, crushing the sweet pink roses, sur-
prising gophers and once a stray coyote—I tried to
talk of crops but could only hear of murders. My
driver had evidently made a study of all murders
in all lands, and by degrees I noticed that the ones
he liked best were the ones that were never found

out. I reflected upon tales I had heard of prairie madness, tales of how the loneliness wears upon some settlers' brain and drives them crazy. I wondered if this young-old man with the blue eyes and odd-sized pupils were going mad. Presently he asked where we were making for. I said "So-and-So's farm." He replied, "Oh! no we're not, I'm taking you for a drive. Where shall we go?" I suggested that the farm would please me best, but he grew argumentative. "I'm not here for work, you know," he drawled presently, "I'm here for my health."

I asked if he was ill, and he said he suffered from brain-storms! Also he said he had noticed me on the train the day before, followed me to the X——, and again to the Board of Trade in the morning. Had heard my business and got the rig to drive me out.

A most enterprising stranger—he must have had plenty of time to spare to alight at a little wayside prairie city for the whim of driving a stray female round for an hour or two!

He was quite amusing, quite courteous. I have never seen or heard of him since; I haven't the least idea if he were really mad or only funny. If he did it all for sport to see what I would do or say he certainly deserves to go in the chapter on artists, for he laid no stress on his alleged brain-trouble, he was most clever, most artistic. If he were really mad why then he still more deserves his place in this chapter, seeing that genius and madness . . . you all know the rest.

I remember once watching a famous English designer of costumes for the stage, Tom Heslewood, worrying out the heraldry of the gowns for the battle scene in *Richard III*. It was very interesting. Here was this scholar, this artist, this man bred of generations of gentlepeople with a mind cultured, fastidious, creative, spending his gifts and time lavishly on the seeming trifle of designing correct heraldic costumes for a scene in a play! I watched his sensitive fingers sketching as he babbled of the murrey and blue, of the House of York, with boar, and the green and white of the House of Tudor, with greyhound, and the dragon dreadful of Cadwallader emitting flames. I asked him why he should bother so much. Very few people can follow the intricacies of heraldic device now-a-days when it has lost general significance, and has grown with successive generations to such involved proportions. He said that I had asked an unintelligent question, that if the audience were made up entirely of heraldic experts he could afford to be careless, they would know better and suffer no harm; but seeing that it would inevitably be composed of people who knew no more of heraldry than myself, he must spare no pains that they should learn nothing inaccurate from his work. I do not know why I have mentioned that conversation, it has no bearing on the thought that was rambling in my mind; it is recorded, I think, because Tom Heslewood's sentiment is one which might with advantage animate us all. Anyway it was a digression. What I was intending to say when I started out was that with the momentum of the history of hundreds of years behind us it would be strange indeed if we had not some Arts. In the slow mills of time Canada will grind out her own civilization, her own expressions of her own history. One can't hurry these things.

As Bliss Carman has it—

Ah! the patience of earth! Look down at the dark pointed firs;
They are carved out of blackness; one pattern recurs and recurs.
They crowd all the gullies and hillsides, the gashes and spurs,
As silent as death. What an image! How Nature avers
The goodness of calm with that taciturn beauty of hers!
As silent as sleep. Yet the life in them climbs and stirs;
They too have received the great law, know that haste but defers
The perfection of time, the initiate gospeller firs!
So year after year, slow ring upon ring they have grown,
Putting infinite long-loving care into leafage and cone.—Etc., etc.

Those lines express beautifully the wisdom, the necessity of patience. Bliss Carman is a delightful singer, I hope he is a Canadian—a lovely trifle is his

> Thought is a garden wide and old
>   For airy creatures to explore,
> Where grow the great fantastic flowers
>   With truth for honey at the core.
> There, like a wild marauding bee,
>   Made desperate by hungry fears
> From gorgeous "If" to dusk "Perhaps"
>   I blunder down the dusk of years.

Though I am determined, in spite of Sir Gilbert Parker, to deny any great literature to Canada "as it leaves me at present," I admit her poet, Robert Service, his place among the minors. And that meek-sounding place is hard to win. Giants there are not yet. They will come.

Robert Service has a certain facility of rhyme and expression; he is what might be called faded Kiplingesque—at moments he stirs. I was asked to talk of Canadian poetry at the London Poets' Club when I returned last autumn, and instead of speaking I asked the President to call on one of the "Expositors" to read out the *Rhyme of the Remittance Man*. It was greeted with favour, the swirl of the line suits the subject, the sonorous voice and fine elocution of the reader wrung every scrap of beauty that was to be wrung from the words. Here is part of the poem:

a certain ignorance of copyright law forbids my
giving the whole of it—

There's a four-pronged buck a-swinging in the shadow of my cabin,
    And it roamed the velvet valley till to-day;
But I tracked it by the river, and I trailed it in the cover,
    And I killed it on the mountain miles away.
Now I've had my lazy supper, and the level sun is gleaming
    On the water where the silver salmon play;
And I light my little corn-cob, and I linger softly dreaming,
    In the twilight, of a land that's far away.

Far away, so faint and far, is flaming London, fevered Paris,
    That I fancy I have gained another star;
Far away the din and hurry, far away the sin and worry,
    Far away—God knows they cannot be too far.
Gilded galley-slaves of Mammon—how my purse-proud brothers
      taunt me!
    I might have been as well-to-do as they
Had I clutched like them my chances, learned their wisdom,
      crushed my fancies,
    Starved my soul and gone to business every day.

While the trout leaps in the river, and the blue grouse thrills
      the cover,
    And the frozen snow betrays the panther's track,
And the robin greets the dayspring with the rapture of a lover,
    I am happy, and I'll nevermore go back.
For I know I'd just be longing for the little old log cabin,
    With the morning-glory clinging to the door,
Till I loathed the city places, cursed the care on all the faces,
    Turned my back on lazar London evermore.

I confess I like Bliss Carman better. A quaint
fantastic imagery hangs about his work; he sings
with a wry smile, a smiling frown. But men of
action prefer Robert Service.

Perhaps if I admit a bias in the matter of painting I may be forgiven for keeping silence about the work of Canadian painters. I know they exist—I have seen some of their pictures. It was my privilege—or misfortune—at one time to be an " art critic," and in that capacity it was my duty to see every picture show in London, a fate which left me stranded on the shores of prejudice so high and dry that " criticism " had to go. I found that I would go any distance to see a caricature by Max Beerbohm, an epic in proportion by James Pryde, a cool study in still life by Nicholson, a portrait by A. E. John or Zuloaga or Howard Somerville, an etching by Whistler; Sargent's odd mingling of carelessness and courage —those unmerciful portraits with sloppy hands pink tipped. One will not see those, I think, much longer; Sargent is painting now to please himself, not to fill the family portrait galleries of Great Britain. He has given up accepting commissions. Such work he is doing!—light problems faced with a courage never attained by any of the French luminists or vibrationists. . . .

I found I would go any distance for those, and almost any distance to avoid the rest!

So, confessing a warped judgment, I mention no Canadian painters.

CHAPTER XI

THE FLY IN THE OINTMENT

WONDERING I have passed from Province to Province. Wondering at the homes to be made, at the husbands to be found, and at the scarcity of women all over the West. That sounds bald, "husbands to be found," unattractively phrased. I will not retract it, nor re-phrase, nor modify. Whatever may be urged to the contrary by the enforced bachelor women of my own land, I know that in their secret hearts most of them think of marriage as the ultimate goal. An honourable wish, by no means to be hidden with shame. Every healthy normal woman has it. If we are in England, as I believe we are, evolving a race of practical neuters we are making for evil, not for good. They are the "oddities" of Kipling's "Mother-hive." Our little Island on the edge of Europe is overcrowded with people, chiefly women, and a vast Continent in North America is at its wits' ends for inhabitants, especially women. Now, why does not plus go over to minus and level things up a little, in order to make both countries more comfortable?

A WOMAN IN CANADA

First one sees in England a surplus of women working hard, working savagely day by day for bread and bacon, working at a ridiculous wage with no hope of ultimate independence, no hope of marriage or motherhood, no hope of anything but the moment's pence for the moment's meal. One sees, too, the middle and upper class women suffering in the press of humans more acutely (because more intelligently) than these, their factory sisters.

Then over here we see a vast majestic country, rich in wine and oil, in bread and bacon, yielding abundantly under cultivation, giving to all who labour with a spendthrift hand. We see the thousands of acres of prairie lying desolate for want of people; the black loam, virgin to the plough, covered with lilies and roses and golden-rod instead of the fruits of the earth—for want of labour. We see the farm homesteads and farmers' wives suffering from lack of servants to cook and mind the house, the farmers themselves frequently leading wretched lives for lack of women to wed. It all sounds so simple of remedy. Wondering and watching I have passed through Canada, telling myself that Englishwomen have never realized the *room* in Canada. There is a wonderful lot of room —room to live in, to be lost in, to make money in;

room to learn the wild ways of the world in, room to cast the fetters of civilization, and room to work —most splendid of all, room to work!

There is room for so many women in the West that the heart aches to see them cramped and struggling there in England; it is paralyzing to travel through both countries and note the crying need in one for the surplus of the other, one is impelled to ask if it is ignorance or cowardice that keeps them away.

And at last I found what I felt all along must exist; a hardship to be faced which makes women justly shrink from the country. First from one prairie wife, and then from another I heard a cry about the hardships of birth on the homesteads. Myself a trained maternity nurse as well as a mother, I know what lack of skilled attention must mean at the hour of travail. And wherever I went I asked how the outlying districts were supplied with midwives. I heard many stories of courage, stories of disaster. One I can never forget, the story of a woman whose first two years on a lonely farm were childless and whose reason began to totter under the stress of loneliness until she found she was to have a baby. The prospect of such an interest changed her life, she was engrossed with hope; it was not possible to obtain a nurse and difficult to get a doctor to the distant homestead, so she and her husband made arrangements for her to go to the nearest hospital forty miles away. She drove over the rough road, the baby was born prematurely and died. I picture her return, to loneliness. I talked with many doctors and nurses, one midwife told me of a case where the lonely young couple found themselves suddenly ushered into parenthood, the nearest doctor was twenty miles away, and they had not been able to get a nurse for love nor money. They were entirely ignorant of obstetric work—the baby was blue and they were frightened. Thereupon, with the placenta unborn, it was put in a hot bath; visions of inverted uterus rise, and appal the initiated. Countless unrecorded cases as terrible must occur. On Pender Island, British Columbia, there are eighty children of school age, so the population must be fairly large. The island has no nurse or doctor. The Jubilee Hospital in Victoria has no maternity wing; at Duncan, on Victoria Island, a district of forty miles is fed by two doctors. The doctor at Davidson in Saskatchewan has a circuit of sixty miles; there are no nurses at Yellowgrass and Wood Mountain; the city hospital at Regina has only three private rooms for maternity cases, in the Catholic Hospital where the Reverend Sister

Superior Mary Duffin and her devoted band of grey
nuns work day and night, there are only four private
rooms, and even they cannot be spared in the Fall
when typhoid is about. These are a few facts and
represent little of the case. Within driving distance
of a city a woman near her confinement may consider herself more or less safe. Some one will be
found to help. But the wives on ranches and farms
at any distance, and there are hundreds of them,
must spend hideous hours looking forward to the
day of trial with every prospect of scrambling
through alone, at the risk of the baby's life as well
as their own, or else relying on the attentions of
some half-breed whose knowledge of the elementary
rules of cleanliness will be less than nothing. The
percentage of lacerations is enormous—one would
expect that under such conditions. Any obstetrician
reading this will realize what I mean when I say
that such neglect leads to the train of evils which
necessitates the building of gynæcological wings on
hospitals. I was filled with concern to learn of the
hardships Canadian mothers are called upon to
endure, I felt I could not ask too many questions to
find out the reason. Doctors, of course, are necessary; wholeheartedly I repeat necessary at confinements, but every doctor and every mother knows

that the nursing which follows after his duties are over have a tremendous part to play in recovery. A woman should not have to drag out a day or two's rest by herself after the doctor has left and then get up and begin her house duties, as many of them do, of those I mean who are lucky enough to get a doctor at all. The maternity nurses I found had in nearly every case gone through the full three or five years' training and were disposed to sniff at maternity work. I can thoroughly understand their point of view. Maternity work is unexciting and very laborious, it is day and night work and very exacting. Fully trained nurses prefer fever or accident work, and when they undertake maternity cases charge exorbitant fees. The general hospitals are in nearly every instance averse to maternity wards. They say, and quite justly, that maternity work should have a separate building and staff.

The prairies suffer greatly in this need of their mothers, but British Columbia even worse, as it is so isolated in settlement and so much more difficult of travel.

I found the nurses were not in every case certain of obtaining their fees, and there was again a difficulty I could understand in the way of meeting this pressing need of maternity assistance; under

stress of fear and love any one can pardon a man
for promising any fee to have his wife tended, and
understand too that with fear allayed and a new
expense safely launched on a slender purse, that
however willing he might delay payment and perhaps need a nurse again before the first obligation
was discharged. A common fee is twenty to twenty-
five dollars a week, and forty or fifty dollars make
a hole, for there are many expenses to think of
besides; the doctor, laundry, travelling and all the
rest. The nurse's point of view has my sympathy
too. She does not want to work hard for a problem-
atical forty dollars when there are plenty of certain
ones to be had. With all these facts before me I
realized one certain thing, that the need of efficient
nurses cried aloud. That it spun from mouth to
mouth never questioned, that no great band of facts
was necessary to back up a plea for attention from
the Government because all in authority know the
need is there. It struck me that the only way to get at
these lone farms was through some subsidized band
of itinerant midwives, a sort of mobile corps unat-
tached to any given town or building, but working
coherently under the direction of the Government.
Women who have thoroughly trained at Queen
Charlotte's Hospital or the Rotunda of Dublin are

capable of undertaking cases unattended by a
doctor, *if need be;* they have not been through the
devastating General Training which, in a very large
percentage of cases in Great Britain, leaves a woman
a gastric invalid with varicose veins, or if it leaves
her healthy nearly always makes her too superior
for maternity work. I hope that does not sound ill-
natured. It is a fact. And one cannot in reason
blame nurses for feeling so when they have given
arduous years to a complete training, and have
emerged fitted to deal with the intensely interesting
inch-by-inch work of fevers and the exciting work
of surgery. Here and there in unfortunate instances
they may get a taste of everything in maternity work,
but fortunately that is comparatively rare. Moreover, as I have already said, the fully trained nurse
wants fully trained fees, and many of the settlers'
wives could not possibly afford them if they could
find an unengaged nurse who was willing to come.
The fully trained nurse also has been through her
purgatory of drudgery in the hospitals, she has
washed and cooked and scrubbed and polished, and
is now a nurse, not a superior ward-maid. Therefore she would be useless practically in the little
prairie shacks where she would have to do all the
domestic work as well as the nursing.

THE FLY IN THE OINTMENT

Looked at from every point of view it seemed to me that the women wanted out West were the qualified midwives trained by such reputable hospitals as I have named. They would accept a reasonable fee of ten dollars a week. At Edmonton I saw the Honourable Mr. Oliver, Minister of the Interior, and put my idea before him. He listened with perfect courtesy, and considered without haste what I said; he admitted the need of such a scheme, but declared finally that he thought it a Provincial rather than a Dominion matter. He said it was the business of the Dominion Government to bring settlers into the country, but the business of the Provincial Governments to look after them when they had once settled.

So I then went to see the Honourable Dr. Rutherford, Premier of Alberta. He also listened very patiently and asked me to put the scheme in writing so that he might submit it in session. He agreed with me that if one Province took up the idea the others would probably fall quickly into line. So I wrote a long letter asking if it would not be possible to establish a body of nurses under Government auspices at every small town or hamlet through the country, from whence they could radiate to the surrounding districts. Such nurses could be guaranteed a minimum fee for every case where the homesteader was unable to pay, and would take ordinary fees in the ordinary way where possible. The homesteader would be under obligation to repay to the Government as soon as possible, and the nurse would not be working for nothing. The nurses in return for such protection would be pledged to take each case in turn as it applied to the office without picking and choosing. The settlers' wives, then, would only need to write in to the nearest branch stating circumstances and asking for a trained midwife at such a date for such a period. I also suggested that no nurse should go to a case for less than twelve days, a useful safeguard for the health of many mothers. Further, I asked if it were not possible that such a body of maternity specialists be attached to the existing order of Victorian Nurses, acting as an endowed Government body, but incorporated with the present order.

I mentioned that in the old country many more women are trained for maternity work than there is work for; and that it should be possible to select from among them women who can bake bread, sew, cook and run a house, women who *knowing the conditions in the West* would be willing to come for the sake of guaranteed employment, and who after settling the patient would turn to and mind the house.

So having heard nothing from Alberta I approached the Premier of British Columbia, who put the matter in council at once, and at least did me the honour to reply. Here is the letter I received—

Provincial Secretary's Office,
Victoria,
15th October, 1908.

" Mrs. George Cran,

"c/o Supt. of Immigration,

"Department of the Interior, Ottawa.

" Madam,

"I beg leave to acknowledge the receipt of your communication of the 9th instant, in which you outline the suggestions offered in your conversation of recent date regarding the bringing of nurses to this Province for extra-hospital work. The matter was laid before the Executive Council at its last meeting, and I am instructed to say that after very careful consideration the Provincial Government feel that they are not in a position to accept suggestions. The matter was thoroughly discussed, and the consensus of opinion was that this being a matter of immigration is one which lies entirely within the province of the Dominion Government at Ottawa.

"I have the honour to be, Madam,

"Your obedient servant,

"H. E. YOUNG

"(Provincial Secretary)."

This was a game of battledore and shuttlecock, the need of the women being the shuttlecock between the greater and lesser governments. I hoped that Saskatchewan might prove more kindly about things, but the Premier was away for the General Election when I reached Regina, and the public health official makes tuberculosis his hobby. He assured me in the airiest way that the women were amply provided for, yet he lives in the province where maternity nurses are scarcest and where one doctor, aforementioned, has a circuit of sixty miles whereon to lavish his attentions. At Winnipeg I was advised to get the municipalities to subsidize the nurses, but my experience of governing bodies inclined me to regard that project with prophetic disappointment, and I went on to Ottawa, where is the head-quarters of the Victorian Order of Nurses, determining to lay the matter before the committee and ask for consideration at its hands.

THE FLY IN THE OINTMENT

The Victorian nurses visit the sick and work, therefore, on short circuits; they, as they exist at present,
are in no way able to meet the need I poignantly
felt to be an urgent one for the widely scattered
mothers of Canada. I saw the committee and de-
tailed my scheme once more, and knew directly I
spoke to the matron that I had met prejudice. The
pity of the whole position is this, that while the fully
trained nurse is more than a trifle scornful of
maternity work, she is violently antipathetic to the
"half-baked" sister, the midwife who has taken
only the short maternity training and is not qualified
for all branches of nursing. I have noticed that
prejudice over and over again, and always with
resentment. They might scorn the maternity nurses
to the crack of doom and welcome if they were
willing to do the work themselves, but they are not.
They oppose the idea of giving maternity nurses a
definite status, and themselves leave the work undone. Meanwhile, the mothers suffer. Any scheme
for alleviating the distress, which none denied, was
unwelcome to the Victorian Order of Nurses. Their
work is great, it is well done, their nurses have
worked hard to get their diplomas and are worthy
of honour. But they met the maternity problem
with prejudice. If an argument is advanced that the

accidents and sicknesses of adults are more important than bringing to birth of the next generation, I
wholly disagree. It is the race that is involved in
maternity work, not the individual. A pregnant
woman is a national asset, a national glory, a national
responsibility. It is the next generation to which
we owe allegiance, should show mercy and consideration, to which we should bend our energies
and skill.

Interfering people are intolerable. They seldom
compass anything. They are always a nuisance.
Frankly I believe I was an interfering person in the
matter of the neglected Western wives. Canada is
not my country, nor was it any of my business to
right its wrongs. I met my deserts. Yet the blood
chills to think of the lonely mother-women, of the
effect on their babes of the unnecessary harshness
of the birth hour and the nervous expenditure in
the anticipation of it. As Mr. Woods of the *Calgary
Herald* said in speaking of the subject, " It grips
one beyond reason."

Her Excellency Lady Grey was good enough to
interest herself in the idea I mooted before the
Victorian Order of Nurses; she mentioned the
Cottage Hospitals sparsely dotted about the prairies
and British Columbia, but realized their inefficiency

in this one particular when I told her how women will come in eighty and a hundred miles for attention to them and yet many hundreds go unattended. Women within possible reach of a doctor, nurse or hospital may be counted provided for, but the women I grieve about are those who can only be reached by such an itinerant body as I have sketched. There are many farmers' wives with children who cannot go to hospital for their confinements as their man is out at work all day and they are unable to leave the house and children. To such women a maternity nurse representing a fortnight's rest would be an inestimable boon.

I am telling English women straightforwardly what to expect at present if they go out and marry on a lonely farm in the North-West. Also I can tell them that every woman who goes out to stay makes it easier for her sisters, for the evil will remedy itself with population. To British women trained at Queen Charlotte's and the Rotunda I would say there is plenty of work to be had if they will take the good and the bad and set about things carefully. It would not be a bad plan to advertise in one or two prairie papers before going out so as to secure one or two cases to go on with and not trust everything to chance. Better still, to find the names of one or two doctors in outlying districts and write direct to them. I hope it has been perfectly clear through all this talk of midwives that I never suggest them as a substitute for doctors, only as allies, and in cases where a doctor is unprocurable by reason of the patient's poverty or distance I maintain that their trained services would be infinitely better for all concerned than those of some terrified ignorant neighbour or dirty half-breed. I beg no one to misapprehend me on this point.

If such British women are prepared to go out and put up with the inconveniences of primitive homesteads, to be housekeeper as well as nurse, and to accept moderate fees—say ten dollars a week—they will find work in plenty. I would recommend them to insist on payment before leaving, and if cash is scarce to take payment in kind—say wheat or live stock. It sounds harsh, but it is only fair to the nurse who may suffer if she has a kind heart and is not armed with stern advice. In the majority of cases her fee would be gladly and punctually paid. A lady whose advice on the subject would be of great value to any one who has courage to face life under such conditions is Miss Benyon of the *Winnipeg Free Press*. She appreciates to the full the dearth of women in the North-West and has many practical hints to offer. There is this to be said, that every maternity nurse who has practised in Canada and marries there will be fully aware of what she is undertaking, and will probably take good care to live within reach of assistance. My sympathies are very much with the English girls who have gone out, reared in that pernicious ignorance of physiological facts which is counted among the many over here for innocence, and has learnt at bitter cost of unnameable suffering the penalties Nature exacts for ignorance—the unforgiveable sin of ignorance.

The care of the lonely mothers, then, as far as I can see, devolves on the individual courage and skill of their British sisters. Had my suggestion found favour with any governing body it would have been a comparatively easy matter to select the suitable women to go out. Any one who knew the North-West could have obtained permission to lecture at the best Maternity Hospitals over here on conditions for nurses out there, and having told in sober truth the whole story the volunteers alone would have been considered, thus eliminating all but those with the desire for pioneer work. From those again the matron would have been asked to remove the names of those below a desired standard in health or efficiency. They would need to be strong, reliable, clever nurses, but if there were a guarantee of steady employment it would be a small matter to get all the picked women needed—steady work is a great attraction to an English nurse.

I do not think government aid would be necessary indefinitely. After a while some of the nurses would make money and start maternity homes here and there; which in their turn would make good training centres for the next generation of nurses, and so the situation would gradually work out of itself. So it will still. Things always do, but meanwhile the women suffer and the children suffer, two sorts of suffering that are exceeding bad for a young race. Canada, so fatherly in its government, so sane and sensible, so wise and patient in most of its measures, is here in this particular extraordinarily callous and short-sighted. All over the country one finds schools, well built, well managed, the scholastic system in Canada is really a remarkable one. Yet it neglects its children at the fountain head of being and hopes for a contented healthy people. I would reverse the system, I would look after them physically first in every possible way, and then set to afterwards with schools and book-learning.

Here I am, then, at the end of all, seeming to say

to women, "Don't go! there are flies in the oint-
ment." But I do not say anything of the sort. To
the right women there is only one word, " Go."

*But the women Canada wants are rare in English
communities.* There is the real trouble.

The English woman is used to large crowds, to a
busy communal life. In Canada she would have to
bring courage for loneliness, she would needs find
companionship in her husband and children, in her
cattle, in the housework, in the very beauty of the
wild itself. The English women are used to
specialized labour; they are artists, or stenographers,
book-keepers, nurses, journalists, dairy-women,
doctors or what not. The Canadian woman will
drive a team of horses when her man is too busy to
work the hayrake or binder, she will be baker, house-
maid, cook, mother, seamstress, nurse to her neighbour five miles off when she is ill, she will run the
dairy, sell the butter and eggs, and keep the farm
accounts all in her own person. The English woman
rises at 7.30 to 9 a.m.; the Canadian woman in the
West at 5 a.m., sometimes earlier, rarely later.

The woman who makes good in Canada is
energetic and brave.

The average English woman is lazy, fond of ease,
and she lacks courage to face new conditions. Now

how to do any good with such a need and such a supply?

In all these large questions one has to speak in masses. The *mass* of English bachelor women is, I am persuaded, unfitted by our complete civilization to face the toils of settlement in a new country. But the exception, the fearless, enthusiastic, clean-bred exception, must exist in her thousands. And to her a direct statement of fact is the strongest appeal. The woman who has faced an unvarnished history of conditions in the country and is still anxious to emigrate is the woman Canada wants.

Let no woman come from England to the Canadian cities; they are over-full already, there is no work for them there, and at best Canadian city life is but a parody of English city life. At the risk of offending I will tell the truth. But if any woman cares for work let her come to the prairies of British Columbia and labour with her hands like the rest. It is a great call for women. There must be some who have the courage and the health to leave the ready-made comforts of the old country, and come into this wild beautiful West, giving their best of mind and body for the race and for the Empire.

CHAPTER XII

THE impertinence of trying to describe Canada in a book, in twenty books, in a lifetime of words! Her people resent it, they can always put up with pæans of praise, but any attempt to find fault annoys them exceedingly; and I agree thus much, that any adverse criticism on any subject should be given out of a sincere heart and intimate knowledge of conditions. In her book *Town and Trail* Mrs. Balmer Watt says—

I suppose that a new country, like a new baby, must patiently submit to a great deal of discussion as to its various characteristics, what the influence of its parentage upon it is, and how far it shows evidence of striking out on an original course. It is the price that it has to pay for the very fact that it is new. In its earliest years it does not mind, being for the most part blissfully unconscious of the attention that is given it. But when, with development, it begins to look forward to the time when it will put away

267

childish things and take its place in the affairs of the world, many of the observations that come in its direction are hardly calculated to put it in a good humour with the kindly disposed people who are responsible for them. It finds itself criticized and advised by those who know the youthful personage they seek to guide so slightly that their interference can only serve to irritate.

This is the stage at which Canada has now arrived. For a long while the people of the Old Land gave little thought to us. To many of her statesmen we were a burden that Britain should get rid of at the earliest opportunity. One prime minister spoke of us as a millstone about the British ratepayer's neck.

All that, of course, has now changed. Hardly a week passes by but we hear of some distinguished Britisher coming out to the Dominion for the purpose of sizing up conditions here. What they have to say when they return home we read with interest, but in very few cases do we find that their observations are of much value to any one concerned.

It would be a matter of great surprise if they were. How can a man who rushes from ocean to ocean and back again in five or six weeks form a proper judgment of the people he has come out to study?

But the man who rushes out and back has his merits, for all the truth in this grievance. He is the looker-on who sees most of the game. That is if he has no prejudices, no affections involved. The biassed writer is always worse than useless. I have heard it said that one writes best of what one is ignorant about, that knowledge cripples and thwarts words. The man is generally chosen to rush over Canada because he is a journalist. And a journalist is an expert in recording. Moreover, he is fresh from the country for which he is going to write, he is able to tell of Canada for those who have not seen it, not from the point of view of those who already live there. After all England is not asking Canadians to come and live in her land, and the big Dominion is calling for settlers all the time. Potential Canadians are not unreasonable in asking to know something of the country before they go to it. So far, then, from resenting talk of herself, why does not Canada encourage more talk in both lands of both her and us? I have referred constantly to the quarrels in which I was involved on that pet grievance of the Canadian—the inferiority of the English settler to every other; the superiority of Canada to England; the coldness of England to her great colony. From first to last that was rammed into my tingling ears. At Saskatoon a melancholy-faced fellow-countryman said to me—

"The Englishman is crucified in Canada."

In justice to Saskatoon I must admit that I could not help feeling that that particular man would be crucified anywhere, he was so melancholy. At Montreal a hospitable native invited me to a royal feast. I was entertained with sumptuous courtesy from every material standpoint, but my host and fellow-guests did not scruple to gibe at the folly of my fellow-Britons till I dissolved in tears and made an ass of myself. But this thing struck me everywhere, that rarely indeed did a Canadian revile England and the English who had been over and seen the old country and its people at first hand. So I have a petition to offer to every Canadian who reads this book, and that is to see Great Britain before condemning it—and till then keep silence. I promise one thing, and that is that no one will suffer the humiliation of hearing his own country derided while he is a guest in ours. English people are immensely interested in Canada, they will ask endless questions, they will listen eternally to talk of it, but I am safe in saying they will not deride unprovoked. It is a pity there is no great Press organ passing between the two countries. If some well-illustrated magazine passed to and fro written by English and Canadian writers equally, I believe a bond of great strength would be established. A great deal of the literature read in the Colony is from the United States—a very great deal of it; an Anglo-Canadian illustrated paper would familiarize readers on both sides with the aspects of either country. On one side we have the great advertising output of the Emigration Bureau and the Canadian Pacific Railway, so that from the commercial aspect we in Great Britain are not unaware of parts of Canada; but we do not advertise our country over the other side, and the untravelled Canadian has the haziest notion only of the land he is loth to admit more powerful than his own. He cannot picture the bustle of our London streets, the thronging masses of people in those vast arteries of commerce. He cannot picture the changes that come into them with every onward impulse of invention—how we ourselves have to grow used to constant change and progress, and learn our London yearly; nothing in the aspect of the City seems constant but its ineffable greys of mist and stone. Daily the aspect of our London is changing; daily old buildings and houses are being levelled to the ground; daily fresh hoardings are pulled down disclosing stately piles and widened spaces.

The noises and the smells of the street are different. As a child I remember coming to London and being struck mightily with the noise of the traffic. It was an insistent roar of clattering hoofs and rolling wheels. Later, coming back to it, I found a difference. It was nearly all the patter of hoofs and jingling of bells. Rubber tyres had come into fashion, and the comparative noiselessness of locomotion which they ensured made it, if not necessary, at least expedient to put bells on the horses' heads. The thrill of the bicycle bell was constantly heard, for cyclists were much more general then than now, and these airy little water spiders of the traffic dodged and darted in a truly alarming fashion among the buses and lighter vehicles. Now-a-days the roar is pitched on a higher note. It is more nerve-racking if less continuous. The noise of London is now a steady series of the diminuendos and crescendos of fast-moving engines, throbbing with the warning hoot of horns. It may be prejudice, but I believe that the ear accepted more kindly the old song of hoof and bell than this present-day clatter of machinery at express speed. Then the smell of the city has changed. One's nostrils are assailed on every hand with the odour of petrol, instead of the former kindly suggestion of a well-ventilated stable.

So, with our environment changing daily, yearly, I believe it would be a good thing to make the Mother Country a visualized fact in the Canadian eye, instead of a dim, meaningless blur. The only comment on the appearance of Great Britain I heard was in Winnipeg, where a man of some imagination said to me one day, " Your country must be like a garden everywhere; it has hedges along the roads and thatched ricks, hasn't it? " (The Canadian never thatches his ricks, the climate makes it unnecessary.) If there could sometimes glow in the Canadian eye a picture of an English village in Shakespeare's country, with the thatched roofs all stained with moss till they have acquired a wonderful nameless colour of age, with the cottage gardens full of hollyhocks and roses, with an old sixteenth-century inn rich in yawning fire-places, beams black with age, oak staircases and walls a yard thick, some such picture mellowed with all the appurtenances of age and history, it would go far to engender pride in the Motherland, far to kill disdain of her acreage.

A WOMAN IN CANADA

I read one day lately in the *Daily Chronicle* a vivid picture of Euston Station, England, at midnight, by Mr. S. R. Littlewood, painted in simple words with a clean touch. I wished, as I read, that that article, illustrated with photographs of the actual scene, could be reproduced in the best Canadian papers. Here is the article—

THE "GOOD-BYE" TRAIN

A FAMILIAR MIDNIGHT SCENE AT EUSTON

In these summer days, when London is preening itself before her myriad guests from oversea, flaunting forth the matchless wealth and glory of the greatest Empire-city that ever was, there are just one or two little scenes in contrast that it is worth while to remember. One means not so much the old, old contrast of rich and poor—of the grey millions on the sunset side of Aldgate pump and the bright, many-coloured life of the West End, overflowing, as M. Guitry described it the other day, with a "splendour of joy."

After all, since Dickens's time, London has never been allowed to forget her poor. It is, moreover, right, natural, and in some ways a new thing, that she should have these moments of exultation over her own beauty; and, to be suré, with the season in its pride, there seems more point than ever in the poet's trope—

To East, the root—to Westward points the flower,
Fair bloom of London, changing hour by hour!

No! The contrast one would emphasize lies simply between welcome and farewell.

It so happens that just in these last few weeks, while distinguished strangers from all quarters of the earth have been revelling in the greeting that only London's opulence can give, certain as yet undistinguished folk have been bidding London good-bye. These are not strangers. They are bred and born Londoners, most of them. But they are going on a far journey—thousands of miles by land and sea —for the simple reason that London, with all its greatness, cannot find room for them.

Let us take the trouble to see them off, and perhaps we shall learn something of the joys and sorrows that lurk beneath the surface of the Cockney panorama. We shall have to make our way to Euston Station just about the time when the theatres are pouring out their cheery throngs of playgoers, and the West End restaurants are filling up for that fatal repast which has to be devoured between half-past eleven and the last bus. Through those gloomy portals we ask our way to the midnight boat-train to Liverpool. There, sure enough, it is, at a remote platform, already crowded with a strangely mingled gathering of men, women and children. This crowd represents—need one say it? —just London's weekly batch of Canadian emigrants, bidding their friends farewell. Nearly all are bound for the far west of the Dominion, starting for the fortnight's journey— third-class and steerage—that will give them their chance of wresting a living from the virgin prairie of Alberta, or British Columbia or Saskatchewan.

They are of all classes—save only the rich. Here are rough labourers in corduroys and knee-straps, white-faced clerks, waiters, mechanics, maids-of-all-work, factory-girls, even middle-aged professional men down on their luck, leaving behind an anxious wife and wondering children, and setting out to essay any new hope that a new world may afford. In the crude, cold light of the arc lamps there is indeed being enacted upon that platform a drama more poignant than any stage could well supply.

The most pathetic feature of it all is, perhaps, the desperate, brave effort at gaiety. While there is still five minutes to spare—though here and there one may see a wife, a mother, a daughter sobbing quietly at the carriage door—the prevailing note is a mad parody of high spirits. Opposite one compartment a bevy of boys and girls are dancing a cake-walk, singing a rag-time tune at the top of their voices, with tears streaming down their cheeks. A little farther down a ring of pals are treating a comrade to "For he's a jolly good fellow," with three times three. One wholly happy episode is to be noted. It is a family send-off to "Grannie," a cheery old lady of nigh seventy. She has been sent for over half the world by a stalwart son who has built a home for himself at last—probably with his own hands—and knows of no better housekeeper for it than his old mother. Everywhere one hears cheery, defiant promises to come back—within a year maybe, or eighteen months—consciously false promises, alas! that the recording angel, let us hope, blots duly from his book.

Soon, and all too inevitably, comes the end—a whistle, a whirlwind of shouts and hoarse cheers, a wild rush to the carriage doors, where all thought of dignity is thrown aside, and bearded men scramble to kiss one another, and husbands and wives cling together on the footboard in a last passionate embrace. Slowly the train grinds its way out, tearing asunder as it goes heaven knows how many hearts, how many bonds of flesh and blood!

Then, when the last gleam of the tail-lights has vanished, and the deadening, blank reaction of it all has come, and the platform is deserted save for little clumps round anguish-stricken women in complete collapse, one is tempted to wonder what really will be the fate of that train-load of humanity, bidden on its way with such yearnings of heart. The women, doubtless, are going to a marriage-market where they will be pretty sure to find themselves at a premium. As for the men, they know grimly enough, some of them, what they are facing. They have been lured by no glamorous dream of the gold-fields, no Bret Harte romance, no whip-crack of an Earl's Court cow-puncher. For these home-steaders of the ultimate wheat-lands, where the man without capital or experience has still, at any rate, some hope, the main ordeal will be just the long, inglorious one of loneliness and monotony. . . .

Perhaps it is well, when one remembers all this, that amongst that little band at Euston not many were callow youths. Most were mature men, who had made the decision of their lives, and whom iron circumstance had already tried and tested, and forced to an understanding of themselves and of their real hopes.

It is a trite saying that the Cockney makes a bad colonist, because he cannot stand the loneliness of the outlying homestead, and drifts to the towns or back to England again. Doubtless this is true in part. One felt somehow that that "jolly good fellow" of the Euston train would probably be returning before many months were over across the unharvested sea. But there are Cockneys, born generally of country-bred parents, who never will be in tune with brick and pavement, flat and "tube"—in whom the land-hunger still survives, eating inward because unsatisfied, like a canker at the heart. Men like these, who have no appetite for the "spoof" ideals that bring fortune in town, and who find that London has but rarely a fair reward for plain honesty and strong arm—men like these are seeking, not their fortune in those Western fields, but life itself.

Not least for the mere onlooker, this little scene of heart-break amidst the flaunting delights of the London season helps to show how wrong is the notion that, because London has become an Imperial city, it has ceased to be above everything the home of its own citizens. After all, to those midnight exiles, London meant no fashionable pageant of park and square and theatre, but some little house in some little row in some little suburb, that held within it what was more to them than all the world beside.

I may seem to be harping on trifles, but I believe the printed word dwells in men's minds, I believe the Press has a great deal to do with directing thought, and I believe that if the Old Country were written of in the Canadian papers in an intimate, descriptive and affectionate way that the people would be drawn insensibly to think of her not as a frigid disdainful autocrat over the seas, but as a beautiful dear old land pursuing a blundering,

honest, generous policy with the kindest will in the world. They would grow to feel her warm obstinate heart beating steadily for them through good report and ill, and learn to lean in trouble and kick in prosperity harder than ever, surer and surer of the Motherland.

*   *   *   *   *   *

Here is the end of the book. The *au revoir* end, because in bones and blood and longing heart I know that somehow, somewhere, I shall again tread and write of that lovely land. What do I remember of Canada now that Quebec has faded away—Quebec with her ramparts and plains, her history, her mighty river—I remember the foaming rapids of Lachine; the enamels; the rolling wheat of the prairies; the fruit orchards of British Columbia and Niagara; the mines of silver, lead, copper, gold; the thrill of the whirling spoon in salmon waters; the cry of a stricken quarry in the bush; the scarlet bunch-berries on the mountains; the snow and the sun and the dominant brilliant sky. I remember these and so much more of loveliness . . . I remember, too, a people given over to work and hope, a people kind and prejudiced and courageous, a great Government which gives its

children schools, experimental farms, free homesteads, a Government which subsidizes the hospitals
so that charity in sickness does not exist, and the
best medical attention may be had of all, a Government which works sanely on commercial lines for
the good of the greatest number, and for all its sense
neglects its women and babes at the hour of birth,
leaving them untended on the outlying homesteads,
a Government which makes at the same time a great
hue and cry about race suicide. I remember these
things.

Every August as harvest comes I must suffer the
restless desire to stand on the prairie and hear again
the rustle of miles of wheat—I shall long to board a
train and lean from the end car to smell the pine
and cedar, to see the silver rails slip from our wheels,
the wooden houses, the great barns, to feel the space,
to lave in silence.

If any woman, reading this, wants to go to a
beautiful country and carve out her own fortune
from its deep loam, I shall be happy to tell all I
can that may help her to Canada, and if that is little
I can at least put her in the way of getting information from the best sources.

There is money to be made there, at farming and
horticulture; at domestic service which entails in

Canada no loss of caste; at maternity nursing; and there are happy homes ahead for many, especially for women who do not settle too far from civilization for safety and comfort.

If I had to earn my living I would go to Canada.

Printed in the United Kingdom
by Lightning Source UK Ltd.
124272UK00001B/204/A